MW01708533

exploring

HEAVENLY PLACES

DREAMSPEAK

VOLUME 8

Hear my words: If there is a prophet among you, I the Lord make myself known to him in a vision; I speak with him in a dream.
Numbers 12:6

Barbara Kain Parker

EXPLORING HEAVENLY PLACES, VOLUME 8
DREAMSPEAK

By Barbara Kain Parker

Published By: Standing in Faith Ministries

Distributed By: Aslan's Place Publications
9315 Sagebrush Street
Apple Valley, CA 92308
760-810-0990
www.aslansplace.com

Edited and formatted by Barbara Kain Parker

Cover Design by Brodie Schmidtke

ISBN # 978-0-9817859-3-6

Printed in the United States of America

EXPLORING HEAVENLY PLACES, VOLUME 8

DREAMSPEAK

Dreamspeak is dedicated to the One who both gives and interprets our dreams. May God use this work to help accomplish His perfect purposes in the life of each reader.

Many are the plans in the mind of a man, but it is the purpose of the Lord that will stand.
Proverbs 19:21

ENDORSEMENT

Dreamspeak is an excellent resource for any believer who desires greater understanding about the practical applications of what God-inspired dreams mean and how they provide divine 'hands-on' assistance in the areas of evangelism, inner healing, deliverance and more.

Barbara Parker has helped me immensely over the years to interpret many of my dreams. She is the 'real deal' and is without question, anointed to speak about this subject matter. She is not only a gifted author but also a dream practitioner who offers keen insight into how 'dreams speak' to everyday issues of the heart. I wholeheartedly recommend this book, as it will speak to you.

Rob Gross
Senior Pastor
Mountain View Community Church
Kaneohe, Hawaii

Table of Contents

FOREWORD

I awake in a panic! What a terrible dream! What could it mean? Different scenarios run through my mind, none of them good. Immediately, I go to my computer, type in the dream and save it in my folder, "Words from the Lord." Next step—attach the document to an email and send it to Barbara Parker. I nervously wait for the interpretation, checking my email frequently. Finally, it arrives in my inbox and I am stunned. She writes, "I think this is a really good dream." "Really?" I think. But as I finish reading the interpretation I know she is right. It was a good dream, even though I had feared the worst.

I could assign many dates to the above situation, for over the years I have found Barbara to have the most amazing and positive dream interpretations I have ever seen. The Lord has gifted her to understand how even the direst components of a dream can be viewed in an encouraging way.

My own dream journey began just after the Lord led me through my first deliverance session in 1989, at Bethany Baptist Church in Montclair, CA. As the dreams increased, I would share them with the participants of our prayer ministry. One friend, Bonnie Jones, would take the dreams and sit before the Lord to inquire about their meaning. The Lord would give her the interpretation, and she would write it down and give it to me. At first I was suspicious, but over time the reality of my Baptist world would confirm time and again both the dream and its interpretation.

Now, twenty-eight years later, I have learned to trust that the Lord really is speaking to me through dreams, and I have realized my dependence on those who have been gifted by the Lord to interpret those dreams. I have been blessed to have many who have interpreted them and have found value in each interpretation, but I must admit that I put the most significance on Barbara's interpretations.

For this reason, she needed to write this book because Barbara brings something new to the literature of dream interpretation. This necessary and important contribution to the mysteries of dreams will provide a framework, which will help you dissect your own dreams so that you can receive encouragement from the Lord as you walk with Him.

Paul L Cox
Aslan's Place

INTRODUCTION

Sweating away at the gym is definitely not my favorite pastime, but often in the midst of my longing to just get finished and leave, the Lord pops ideas into my head. On this day it was, "Write a book about dream interpretation for the *Exploring Heavenly Places* series." There was a spark of excitement at the thought, but I had to ask, "Who, me? Write about dreams? What would I write, Lord? What can be said that has not already been written? You know there are already lots of resources available about dream interpretation, many of which are on my bookshelf, and most are very much the same."

After running the idea by Paul Cox (he liked it!), I explained to the Lord that I was willing, but I would need to rely on Him for inspiration so the book wouldn't read like a re-tread. I shouldn't have been surprised that He immediately began providing ideas.

Why would Dreamspeak be included in a series about heavenly places? The answer is simple, yet complex. Dreams and visions occur outside of the dimensions to which we are accustomed, and in them we get a taste of what it is like not to be bound by time and space; we have experiences that are seemingly impossible from an earthly perspective; we are allowed opportunities to see into the invisible spiritual realms and interact with God there.

Whether one's interest stems from Christianity, New Age thought, or just idle curiosity, dream interpretation is a popular topic. Therefore, in the vast array of resources that are available, it's very important for Christians to view dream interpretation only from a Biblical perspective to accurately discern the Lord's meaning of these night parables. His perspective is the only one that counts!

This book is about my personal journey into dream interpretation. It's much more of a this-is-how-God-does-it-with-me account than a one-size-fits-all instruction manual, which I hope will encourage others to venture out into the heavenly realms of dream exploration and interpretation.

That said, at the end of each chapter is a practical application that can be used to begin building a foundation for dream interpretation in one's life. These practical applications are also summarized in Appendix 2.

Happy dreaming!

Barbara Kain Parker
Standing in Faith Ministries

CHAPTER ONE
DREAMSPEAK

For several months I wondered what the sub-title of this book should be, but nothing seemed to work. Should it be the same as my webinar, *Unraveling the Mystery of Dream Interpretation*?[1] No, that's accurate, but it wasn't quite right. Finally, in a 'suddenly' moment, the Holy Spirit whispered, "*Dreamspeak*".

Dreamspeak is a term that is often used in regard to the symbolism of dreams and visions, but my favorite definition comes from Paul Cox, who responded to a text informing him that the Lord had provided the sub-title with, "Yeah, the language that only you and God know." So true! God communicates with each person in a unique and highly individualized way; and while there are a lot of commonalities, there is no one-size-fits-all method to understand exactly what He is saying every single time. Dreamspeak is the pictorial, one-on-one language of dreams and visions in which God speaks privately to you, and you alone; though on occasion He may give the interpretation to someone else, as He often did with Joseph and Daniel:

> *And Pharaoh said to Joseph, "I have had a dream, and there is no one who can interpret it. I have heard it said of you that when you hear a dream you can interpret it." Joseph answered Pharaoh, "It is not in me; God will give Pharaoh a favorable answer."* [2]

> *Daniel answered the king and said, "No wise men, enchanters, magicians, or astrologers can show to the king the mystery that the king has asked, but there is a God in heaven who reveals mysteries…A great God has made known to the king what shall be after this. The dream is certain, and its interpretation sure."* [3]

Accurate dream interpretation comes from God, and anyone who claims they can <u>always</u> interpret dreams, either on their own or by using a particular method, should be viewed with a healthy dose of skepticism. Even the most gifted dream interpreter should not be surprised if some dreams are not understood, because God's ways are surely beyond finding out:

> *For as the heavens are higher than the earth, so are my ways higher than your ways and my thoughts than your thoughts.*[4]

Practical Application:

Start identifying your personal Dreamspeak vocabulary by writing down your observations, including such things as symbols, people who appear, repetitious dreams, common themes, and anything else that occurs to you.

1 Available at: http://aslansplace.com/language/en/unraveling-the-mystery-of-dream-interpretation-barbara-parker/

2 Genesis 41:15-16

3 Daniel 2:28-29a, 45b

4 Isaiah 55:9

CHAPTER TWO
PARABLES IN THE NIGHT

It was mid-2000, and I was desperate. My only child had gone off to college and rarely came home, so empty-nest syndrome was kicking in big time. One day while channel surfing, I encountered a woman's testimony that would change my life:

> A high school dropout, she married at fourteen, was deserted twice by her teenage husband during the first six months of their life together, gave birth to her first child at fifteen, and failed at two more marriages before finally wedding the man with whom she would grow old. She found fame and fortune; yet she endured unimaginable heartache, losing one daughter with Down's Syndrome to encephalitis, another to a bus accident that occurred while on a mission trip to Tijuana, and an eighteen-year-old son to a tragic accident while he served in the military in Germany. Yet there she sat in her wheelchair, a grand old lady whose gentle smile belied her deteriorating health and the recent loss of her husband of fifty-one years. The television interviewer asked, "What does Jesus mean to you?" And the 'Queen of the West', Dale Evans, literally seemed to glow as she answered, "Why he's my best friend—he's right here with me all of the time," gesturing to her side as if Jesus were physically standing there.

The calm, peaceful certainty with which she spoke pierced my heart as I wondered what was wrong with me. I'd been a Christian since I was eight years old and had only experienced such closeness with God a few times, and those had been long ago. My journey to a deeper, more intimate relationship with my Lord began at that moment as I began to pursue Him relentlessly.

It was hard. Along with a renewed commitment to God came a refining furnace[1] that was hotter than anything I could ever have imagined, and for six-plus years I learned first-hand the importance of the Apostle Paul's words:

> *Not only that, but we rejoice in our sufferings, knowing that suffering produces endurance, and endurance produces character, and character produces hope, and hope does not put us to shame, because God's love has been poured into our hearts through the Holy Spirit who has been given to us.*[2]

Though I'd been in church throughout most of my life I'd never received any good teaching about how to develop intimacy with God; in fact, I'd never even heard about it. As a result, my journey was very much a do-it-yourself project that included a lot of trial and error.

One of my first steps toward intimacy was journaling, and as time went by an unusual pattern developed, with many entries including a parable that illustrated an observation. Repeated questions to the Lord about why I found myself writing parables went unanswered. Would these become articles or books? As it turned out, many of them did; but any concept of dream interpretation had not yet appeared on my radar, so God's personalized introductory course to understanding His night parables went un-recognized for several years.

Along with journaling, I dug into Bible study deeper than ever before and began buying and soaking up book after book about the Holy Spirit and prophetic ministry, two more subjects that hadn't been covered in my conservative Baptist upbringing. Gradually climbing out of my rigid theological box, something else began happening: dreams, and seemingly significant ones at that; but for the most part I was still clueless about what they meant. Fortunately, I started writing some of them down.

In January 2005, my husband and I came to Aslan's Place for a ministry school with no idea of what to expect. The first morning, Paul said the Lord had placed an angel in front of each person so we could practice discernment, and my wall of skepticism went right up; but a few moments later I was feeling an angel, and life changed forever. I felt like I'd finally come home, and was so excited that I began hanging out around Aslan's Place at every opportunity. It didn't take long to realize the importance of dreams, so I delved into more books, seminars, and workshops to learn as much as possible about how God speaks during the night. What a relief it was to learn that sleeping, which used to seem like such a waste of time, is actually a very active interlude in which our spirits interact with the Spirit of God!

Think about it, in our dreams we can have literal, life changing encounters with God, and isn't that what we desire most?

Practical Application:

Pursue intimacy with God as relentlessly as you would pursue a potential love interest. Talk to Him, walk with Him, listen to Him; learn to recognize and understand His voice any time of the day or night, whether awake or asleep.

[1] Isaiah 48:10

[2] Romans 5:3-5

CHAPTER THREE
CONVERSATIONS

Any parent or grandparent is well acquainted with the adorable and often humorous process of a toddler learning to talk, and many will gladly regale any audience with stories of their brilliant offspring. I quickly admit that I'm no exception, so forgive me for gushing. My identical twin granddaughters are cuter than cute, and some of their cutest moments (well documented on videos, of course!) have been early conversations with one another. Chattering away with words largely indecipherable to anyone else, they seemed to understand each other perfectly and clearly enjoyed their intimate conversations.

> Conversation is a form of interactive, spontaneous communication between two or more people. Typically, it occurs in spoken communication.[1]

It is apparent that God also enjoys a good talk, as His conversations with man are recorded over and over throughout the Bible. Occasionally, they occur in face-to-face encounters, as with Adam and Eve,[2] Abraham,[3] or Moses:

> *Thus the LORD used to speak to Moses face to face, as a man speaks to his friend.*[4]

More often though, God's conversations with mankind were recorded in dreams and visions, as in His familiar exchange with Solomon:

> *At Gibeon the Lord appeared to Solomon in a dream by night, and God said, "Ask what I shall give you." And Solomon said, "You have shown great and steadfast love to your servant David my father, because he walked before you in faithfulness, in righteousness, and in uprightness of heart toward you...Give your servant therefore an understanding mind to govern your people, that I may discern between good and evil, for who is able to govern this your great people?" It pleased the Lord that Solomon had asked this. And*

> *God said to him, "Because you have asked this, and have not asked for yourself long life or riches or the life of your enemies, but have asked for yourself understanding to discern what is right, behold, I now do according to your word…And Solomon awoke, and behold, it was a dream.*[5]

Solomon wasn't the only one who spoke with God in this manner, and it is clear that Dreamspeak has long been a favored method of communication for Him:

> *And God spoke to Israel in visions of the night and said, "Jacob, Jacob." And he said, "Here I am."*[6]

> *Now there was a disciple at Damascus named Ananias. The Lord said to him in a vision, "Ananias." And he said, "Here I am, Lord."*[7]

Jacob and Ananias understood such God encounters, and both responded to Him by saying, "Here I am," almost as naturally as we would say hello to a friend when answering a phone. Their responses were born out of intimacy—out of long, faith-filled relationships. But that was then and this is now, so does God still speak this way? Yes!

Foundational questions settle the issue. Does God change? No:

> *Jesus Christ is the same yesterday and today and forever.*[8]

> *For I the LORD do not change…*[9]

Is there anything in the Bible suggesting that His presence and power as experienced in the New Testament could not be possible in any generation? No.

> *Every good gift and every perfect gift is from above, coming down from the Father of lights, with whom there is no variation or shadow due to change.*[10]

Is there anything in the Bible that suggests He only speaks through dreams to select people? No. It's clear biblically that believers and non-believers, young and old, rich and poor, kings and slaves, Jews and Gentiles can encounter God:

> *So Peter opened his mouth and said: "Truly I understand that God shows no partiality...*[11]

Scripture is also clear that dreams and visions will only increase, not decrease, as time goes by:

> *And it shall come to pass afterward, that I will pour out my Spirit on all flesh; your sons and your daughters shall prophesy, your old men shall dream dreams, and your young men shall see visions.*[12]

In one very memorable dream from 2005, I had been talking with a nice looking young man with curly red hair. The conversation was so pleasant and informative that I was very disappointed when the man got up to leave. He seemed to understand though; and as he was walking away he turned and said, "Don't worry; I'll be around. I'm not immaterial you know." More dream scenes followed and when I finally woke up I wondered who he was and what his unusual comment meant. However, new to dream interpretation, it took a very long time to fully understand that this was Jesus, apparently looking very much like the son of David, who was very likely a redhead.[13]

He definitely is still around! He invisibly walks and talks with me everyday, and occasionally appears in my dreams. Like the two who met Him on the Road to Emmaus, I don't always recognize Him in the moment; but once awake I can easily relate to their experience:

> *And their eyes were opened, and they recognized him. And he vanished from their sight. They said to each other, "Did not our hearts burn within us while he talked to us on the road, while he opened to us the Scriptures?"*[14]

After the surprise encounter with Jesus, the two immediately hurried back to Jerusalem to share the exciting news. Likewise, we can expect to be blessed when He shows up for a talk in our dreams.

Practical Application:

Ponder and pray about dream encounters with an unidentified man (often, the Lord) to determine if you have had one-on-one conversations with the Lord while you slept.

[1] https://en.wikipedia.org/wiki/Conversation

[2] Genesis 2

[3] Genesis 18

[4] Exodus 33:11a

[5] Excerpts from 1 Kings 3:5-15

[6] Genesis 46:2s

[7] Acts 9:10

[8] Hebrews 13:8

[9] Malachi 3:6

[10] James 1:17

[11] Acts 10:34

[12] Joel 2:28

[13] 1 Samuel 16:12 Complete Jewish Bible (CJB)

[14] Luke 24:31-32

CHAPTER FOUR

MY TAKE ON DREAMS

The dream books on my shelf multiplied, and I collected list after list of metaphors from various authors to develop a personal vocabulary list of symbols, colors, and numbers; finally settling on a few favorite books that I still refer to quite often. As alluded to initially, there's a lot of repetition amongst dream resources; but through gleaning a little bit here and a little bit there, my personal 'take' on dreams emerged.

I believe that dreams should be viewed from a positive perspective; and they are for the purpose of building us up, not tearing us down. After all, God's agenda is never to terrorize but to encourage, deliver, and heal. He earnestly wants to reach in and speak to our hearts, bringing each person into a place of wholeness in and through the Lord Jesus.

> *For in him the whole fullness of deity dwells bodily, and you have been filled in him, who is the head of all rule and authority.*[1]

"But, but, but... What if, what if, what if???" I can hear the questions already. What if it's a nightmare and I wake up drenched in sweat and scared to death? What if it's an embarrassing scenario? What if it seems to be disturbing news? We'll talk more about all that later, but for now just remember that fear should be always removed from the interpretation equation. Even if things look bad, God's purposes are always good; and the outcome of a seemingly terrible dream can always be handled through prayer as we submit it to Him and receive His peace. Remember Jesus' promise:

> *But the Helper, the Holy Spirit, whom the Father will send in my name, he will teach you all things and bring to your remembrance all that I have said to you. Peace I leave with you; my peace I give to you. Not as the world gives do I give to you. Let not your hearts be troubled, neither let them be afraid.*[2]

Isn't it both an amazing and comforting thought that God communicates with us while we sleep? Think about it; during our waking hours we get so caught up in our daily lives that it is way too easy to forget to listen for the Lord's input. So, in His infinite wisdom, God talks to us when we are not otherwise occupied. He picks a time when our body is at rest and our spirits are wide open to receive, a time when our logical human thought processes yield to the Holy Spirit instead of ignoring or arguing with Him.

> *For God may speak in one way, or in another,*
> *Yet man does not perceive it.*
> *In a dream, in a vision of the night,*
> *When deep sleep falls upon men,*
> *While slumbering on their beds,*
> *Then he opens the ears of men,*
> *And seals their instruction.*[3]

In other words, even if we don't recall a thing, we can be assured that He has placed His messages of instruction, encouragement, prophecy, or revelation within our spirits. In 2004, I journaled about a dream that illustrates this:

> I was writing down a previous dream in my journal. Some of it was in regular ink and some was invisible ink so does this indicate some things are hidden and yet to be revealed?

Remember, God is actually speaking all of the time if we pay attention. Since we may hear from Him during either our waking or sleeping hours, it seems wise throughout each day to consider the question about the circumstances of daily living, "If this was a dream, what would it mean?" Conversely, we can carry our dreams over from darkness into daylight by asking, "Since this is a dream, how does it apply to my life?"

God's reasons for conversing with us in dreams are often listed in helpful categories in many dream resources. Though valid, I hesitate to reproduce such lists here because my goal is to encourage out-of-the-box thinking and to place no limits on the creative ways that God may choose to speak.

> *Oh, the depth of the riches and wisdom and knowledge of God! How unsearchable are his judgments and how inscrutable his ways! For who has known the mind of the Lord, or who has been his counselor?* [4]

> *But, as it is written, "What no eye has seen, nor ear heard, nor the heart of man imagined, what God has prepared for those who love him"— these things God has revealed to us through the Spirit. For the Spirit searches everything, even the depths of God. For who knows a person's thoughts except the spirit of that person, which is in him? So also no one comprehends the thoughts of God except the Spirit of God. Now we have received not the spirit of the world, but the Spirit who is from God, that we might understand the things freely given us by God. And we impart this in words not taught by human wisdom but taught by the Spirit, interpreting spiritual truths to those who are spiritual.*[5]

That said, since this is a how-He-does-it-with-me account I will share some of my own dreams as we go along that will illustrate not only various types of dreams, but also how His ultimate purpose is always good.

> *In him we have obtained an inheritance, having been predestined according to the purpose of him who works all things according to the counsel of his will, so that we who were the first to hope in Christ might be to the praise of his glory.*[6]

Practical Application:
Begin learning your own personal dream language by recording your dreams in whatever format works best for you (searchable databases are helpful). Consider the themes, people, and symbols that appear and pray about what they mean to you.

[1] Colossians 2:9-10

[2] John 14:26-27

[3] Job 33:14-16
[4] Romans 11:33-34
[5] 1 Corinthians 2:9-13
[6] Ephesians 1:11-12

CHAPTER FIVE
DIMENSIONALITY

In a dream world, nothing is impossible and we may find ourselves traveling though time, walking on water, breathing under water, flying though the air in a car, or floating thorough walls. Images may morph from one thing into another; or we may also find ourselves experiencing or viewing several scenes at once, multitasking in ways that far exceed our physical capabilities. Familiar laws of physics do not apply as gravity disappears, animals speak, inanimate objects dissolve, and we pass through portals or star gates. We may discover that we are both observing and participating at the same time, experiencing the action but also watching ourselves as if in a movie; and what previously seemed like science fiction becomes reality. Our experiences in heavenly dimensions rival anything found in such fictional tales as *Star Wars, Alice in Wonderland, The Neverending Story, Chronicles of Narnia,* or any of the plethora of television shows and movies that breach the limits of day-to-day life in our familiar world.

Ah, but that's all science fiction; or so we thought. If our dreams really are undeniably inter-dimensional experiences there's got to be biblical evidence. And there is!

> *And he dreamed, and behold, there was a ladder set up on the earth, and the top of it reached to heaven. And behold, the angels of God were ascending and descending on it!* [1]

Sent away by his parents to find a wife in Canaan, and escaping the wrath of his brother after receiving the family birthright and blessing, Jacob had settled down for the night when he encountered the heavenly realms in a dream. Nŏt only did he witness a portal into the heavens and see angels coming and going, but he also had a face-to-face encounter with God that shook him to his core:

> *And behold, the Lord stood above it and said, "I am the Lord, the God of Abraham your father and the God of Isaac. The land on*

> *which you lie I will give to you and to your offspring. Your offspring shall be like the dust of the earth, and you shall spread abroad to the west and to the east and to the north and to the south, and in you and your offspring shall all the families of the earth be blessed. Behold, I am with you and will keep you wherever you go, and will bring you back to this land. For I will not leave you until I have done what I have promised you." Then Jacob awoke from his sleep and said, "Surely the Lord is in this place, and I did not know it." And he was afraid and said, "How awesome is this place! This is none other than the house of God, and this is the gate of heaven."*[2]

Ezekiel, physically living among the Israelite captives in Babylon, was shown literal events that were occurring in Jerusalem:

> *In the sixth year, in the sixth month, on the fifth day of the month, as I sat in my house, with the elders of Judah sitting before me, the hand of the Lord God fell upon me there...He put out the form of a hand and took me by a lock of my head, and the Spirit lifted me up between earth and heaven and brought me in visions of God to Jerusalem, to the entrance of the gateway of the inner court that faces north, where was the seat of the image of jealousy, which provokes to jealousy.*[3]

Daniel experienced dreams and visions of the end times that included not only terrifying events but also the Ancient of Days heavenly court in session. Like Ezekiel, these heavenly experiences were so real that they left him shaken physically:

> *In the first year of Belshazzar king of Babylon, Daniel saw a dream and visions of his head as he lay in his bed. Then he wrote down the dream and told the sum of the matter... "As I looked, thrones were placed, and the Ancient of Days took his seat; his clothing was white as snow, and the hair of his head like pure wool; his throne was fiery flames; its wheels were burning fire. A stream of fire issued and came out from before him; a thousand thousands served him, and ten thousand times ten thousand stood before him; the court sat in judgment, and the books were opened...Here is the end of the matter. As for me, Daniel, my thoughts greatly alarmed me, and my color changed, but I kept the matter in my heart."*[4]

> *In the third year of the reign of King Belshazzar a vision appeared to me, Daniel, after that which appeared to me at the first. And I saw in the vision; and when I saw, I was in Susa the citadel, which is in the province of Elam. And I saw in the vision, and I was at the Ulai canal...And I, Daniel, was overcome and lay sick for some days. Then I rose and went about the king's business, but I was appalled by the vision and did not understand it.*[5]

Paul experienced inter-dimensionality on the Road to Damascus when he personally encountered Jesus, who had already ascended into heaven. Years later, he wrote to the Corinthians:

> *I have to boast, even though it doesn't do any good. But I will now talk about visions and revelations given me by the Lord. I know a certain Christian man who fourteen years ago was snatched up to the highest heaven (I do not know whether this actually happened or whether he had a vision—only God knows). I repeat, I know that this man was snatched to Paradise (again, I do not know whether this actually happened or whether it was a vision—only God knows), and there he heard things which cannot be put into words, things that human lips may not speak.*[6]

Evidence is clear throughout the Bible that dreams and visions are supernatural excursions into the heavenly places, and since God never changes, we can be assured that our experiences today are just as valid as they would have been thousands of years ago. I am so very grateful for God's written proof so I can know for certain that my own inter-dimensional 'road trips', some of which I'll share below, are not simply figments of my imagination.

One night the dream sequences had flowed from one scene to another, until I finally found my self in a room alone with my husband and another man who I knew to be an angel. Suddenly, I realized I was floating face down toward to the floor. The next thing I knew, the man was helping me to my feet and saying, "You've been gone for three days." I awoke startled, but with a certainty that I had indeed traveled somewhere outside of my time and space for three literal days. Back or forward in time, I don't know; destination, I don't know; but I won't be surprised at all if someone comes up to me one day and asks, "Remember when we..."

It's not uncommon for my dreams to involve Aslan's Place since the Lord has miraculously interwoven my life and ministry with that of Paul and Donna Cox. While dreaming of attending a seminar with friends at Aslan's Place, I suddenly found myself, along with several other people, transported to a barren, remote location beside a lonely road with the wind blowing ferociously. Instantly, I knew what had happened and wondered if this was not only another place but also another time. The experience was vivid and felt very real. Wondering how we were to get back, I entered into dream mode again and through one scene after another, the Lord proved His sufficiency by providing all that was needed. Just before waking, I found myself back where I'd started.

We often pray the Lord's Prayer, asking for God's kingdom to come on earth as it is in heaven, but His kingdom is an unseen, spiritual one for the most part. In our dreams and visions, He graciously takes us into those invisible dimensions where He reveals His mysteries within our hearts.

Practical Application:
Consider the dimensionality of your dreams. Where have you gone? What have you experienced? Did your experience seem historical or futuristic?

[1] Genesis 28:12

[2] Genesis 28:13-17

[3] Ezekiel 8:1, 3

[4] Daniel 7:1, 9-10, 28

[5] Daniel 8:1-2, 27

[6] 2 Corinthians 12:1-4

CHAPTER SIX

POOF, AND IT'S GONE!

Tourist traps abound as one travels just about anywhere in the world. On road trips through the southwestern deserts of the United States these may take the form of gift shops that are advertised miles in advance. Most of them are a huge disappointment by the time one arrives but by then you're so ready for a bathroom break that you stop anyway. Inside, one usually finds a large variety of items of regional interest, though a close inspection will reveal that they are made in China or some other far-away land more often than not. Prominently displayed are the beautiful dream catchers, originally created by First Nations peoples who believed that the night air is filled with both good and bad dreams and that a dream catcher hanging over or near the bed and swinging freely in the air would catch those dreams as they flow by. Good dreams supposedly know how to slip through the holes and slide down the soft feathers so gently that many times the sleeper does not know that he/she is dreaming. On the other hand bad dreams don't know the way and get tangled in the web, perishing with the first light of the new day. Nice, if it really worked, but it doesn't!

It was eighth grade, and I'd had the most incredible dream ever, one I would never forget! Such a great plot; complete with everything necessary to finally get an A the next time our English teacher delivered the dreaded news that we had to write a story. Other writing assignments were fine, but coming up with an interesting story line was beyond me; so I remember very clearly the moment a few months later when the previously dreaded assignment was given. In shock, I sat helplessly at my desk with absolutely no memory of my award-winning dream. Too bad that nobody had ever taught me the truth of scripture:

> *He will fly away like a dream and not be found; he will be chased away like a vision of the night.*[1]

Moses understood the transitory nature of dreams. In praying about the brevity of life, he compared it to a quickly vanishing dream:

> *For a thousand years in your sight are but as yesterday when it is past, or as a watch in the night. You sweep them away as with a flood; they are like a dream, like grass that is renewed in the morning: in the morning it flourishes and is renewed; in the evening it fades and withers.*[2]

Fortunately, Daniel understood too. Had he not, would he have been able to recall the details of his dream/visions of the four beasts?

> *In the first year of Belshazzar king of Babylon, Daniel saw a dream and visions of his head as he lay in his bed. Then he wrote down the dream and told the sum of the matter.*[3]

We don't need dream catchers, but we do need to catch our dreams by following Daniel's example.

Practical Application:

Develop a habit of writing down your dreams as soon as you wake up.

[1] Job 20:8

[2] Psalm 90:4-6

[3] Daniel 7:1

Chapter Seven
Unforgettable

When it comes to dreams, we're not at all like fictional Detective Carrie Wells of TV's four-season crime drama, *Unforgettable*, who never forgot anything she'd seen due to an unusual condition known as hyperthymesia. [1] But to quote my friend Paul Cox, "Nothing is always;" so it should be mentioned that there are exceptions to the general rule that dreams fade quickly, such as the one we find in the life of the Egyptian Pharaoh:

> *Pharaoh dreamed that he was standing by the Nile, and behold, there came up out of the Nile seven cows, attractive and plump, and they fed in the reed grass. And behold, seven other cows, ugly and thin, came up out of the Nile after them, and stood by the other cows on the bank of the Nile. And the ugly, thin cows ate up the seven attractive, plump cows. And Pharaoh awoke. And he fell asleep and dreamed a second time. And behold, seven ears of grain, plump and good, were growing on one stalk. And behold, after them sprouted seven ears, thin and blighted by the east wind. And the thin ears swallowed up the seven plump, full ears. And Pharaoh awoke, and behold, it was a dream. So in the morning his spirit was troubled, and he sent and called for all the magicians of Egypt and all its wise men. Pharaoh told them his dreams, but there was none who could interpret them to Pharaoh.*[2]

It appears that Pharaoh's dreams were so disturbing and memorable that he apparently didn't need to write them down, and could easily recount them word for word.

We may also experience such dreams on occasion; dreams that are seared into our mind so clearly that they will never fade. When this occurs we can be certain of one thing—it's important.

Pharaoh's dreams were prophetic warnings of a coming famine and had he not pursued the interpretation the result would have been disastrous, with multitudes dying of starvation. Fortunately, his dilemma was solved when Joseph interpreted the dreams and preparations could be made.

Unforgettable dreams may range from personal to global in scope; their nature may be all over the board; from prophetic, to calling, to deliverance, to comfort, to instruction, to intercession, to whatever else it is that God wants you to know.

On January 20, 2004, I had an intense dream that didn't quickly fade away. For a long time I wondered what it could mean but only understood its prophetic nature after-the-fact, about a year later. Not being a big sports fan, it was quite unusual that I dreamed about watching a football game on TV with a group of people, rooting for one team because I didn't like the other for some unknown reason. The odd thing was that the game went very quickly, with the time clock counting down very fast for each quarter as if time itself had been speeded up, so the whole game was almost over shortly after it began. A few minutes from the end of the fourth quarter the screen went blank, as if all connections had been severed and there was nothing left but static. Somehow we knew there had been a tremendous explosion, perhaps on the level of a nuclear bomb in Southeast Asia. There was immediate speculation regarding what had just happened, what would happen next, what the reaction of other countries would be, and immediate criticism of the USA for not moving quickly enough to help.

Sometime in early 2005, I thought about the dream and realized it had been prophetic of the 9.2 magnitude earthquake that occurred in the Indian Ocean on December 26, 2004, and triggered the terribly destructive Indonesian tsunami. To review that event, it was the third-largest earthquake ever recorded on a seismograph, had the longest duration of faulting ever observed (between 8.3 and 10 minutes), caused the entire planet to vibrate as much as 1 centimeter (0.4 inches), and triggered other earthquakes as far away as Alaska. Internationally, more than fourteen billion US dollars were donated in humanitarian aid.[3]

In my dream, the game clock represented the four quarters of the year, and the explosion that happened in the last few minutes of the countdown foreshadowed the earthquake, which occurred only five days from the end of the fourth quarter of 2004. Relatively speaking, there were only minutes to go before New Years Day. The impact was so severe and far reaching it could certainly be compared to the power of a nuclear explosion—consider the lesser impact of a 6.5 earthquake in Afghanistan during 1998, which released energy equivalent to a 2000-kiloton nuclear explosion.[4] Finally, within a very short time of the earthquake and tsunami, news reports were full of accusations that the USA had not responded with aid quickly enough.

As it happens, both Pharaoh's dream and mine were prophetic in nature, revealing God's ability to see what is yet to come in our future. Other unforgettable dreams may occur for a variety of reasons and while we cannot be certain the biblical dreamers didn't write them down, it's probably a sure bet that both Abimelech and Pilate's wife remembered what God had to say during their sleep:

> *But God came to Abimelech in a dream by night and said to him, "Behold, you are a dead man because of the woman whom you have taken, for she is a man's wife." Now Abimelech had not approached her. So he said, "Lord, will you kill an innocent people? Did he not himself say to me, 'She is my sister'? And she herself said, 'He is my brother.' In the integrity of my heart and the innocence of my hands I have done this." Then God said to him in the dream, "Yes, I know that you have done this in the integrity of your heart, and it was I who kept you from sinning against me. Therefore I did not let you touch her. Now then, return the man's wife, for he is a prophet, so that he will pray for you, and you shall live. But if you do not return her, know that you shall surely die, you and all who are yours."*[5]

> *Besides, while he [Pilate] was sitting on the judgment seat, his wife sent word to him, "Have nothing to do with that righteous man, for I have suffered much because of him today in a dream."*[6]

It's probable that any of us who heard the Lord saying in a dream, "Behold, you're a dead man," would be unlikely to forget it either! As for Pilate's wife, there is no record of exactly what she experienced; it could have been a warning such as with Abimelech, or it could have been about her own need for God. Whatever the case, she "suffered much", and probably remembered the dream her entire life.

Whatever the message, unforgettable dreams are undoubtedly important and come with a God-given opportunity for insight into spiritual matters, personal direction, prophetic vision of things only God can see, comfort, and rest; the list is as endless as are God's reasons for having these conversations in the night that are seared into our memories.

Practical Application:

Write down any vivid dreams that you have never forgotten, and begin praying about what they might mean. Also, even if a dream seems like one you will never, ever, forget; write it down anyway because you just might.

[1] A condition of possessing an unusually detailed memory of autobiographical events

[2] Genesis 41:1-8

[3]https://en.wikipedia.org/wiki/2004_Indian_Ocean_earthquake_and_tsunami

[4] https://www2.usgs.gov/faq/categories/9839/3338

[5] Genesis 20:3-5

[6] Matthew 27:19

CHAPTER EIGHT
IT BEARS REPEATING

Repetition is another key principle of Dreamspeak. When a dream is repeated, whether exactly or in a similar fashion, we can be certain it is important. However, unlike an exasperated parent who cries in frustration, "How many times do I have to tell you to..." or, "Don't make me tell you again," God patiently keeps sending similar dreams over and over and over until we finally pay attention and find out what they mean. Pharaoh's two dreams, interpreted by Joseph to be about the impending seven years of plenty to be followed by seven years of famine, is a great example.[1]

Perhaps, like me, you've had repetitious dreams over the years but never knew they were important messages from God. In retrospect, I can see that when I was a teenager, He was already speaking to me about events that wouldn't even begin to occur for many years to come.

If you're old enough to remember George Reeves and the *Adventures of Superman* on a 1950's black-and-white TV, you'll probably recall that a little jump would propel him into the air as he soared off into the skies on his continual quest for justice. In one of my repeating dreams, a similar jump would launch me into the air, but instead of zooming off "faster than a speeding bullet", I would float around my neighborhood, looking down on rooftops and observing whatever was happening. Little did I know that flying dreams indicate an ability to 'fly' high in the Spirit; little did I know that many years later I would co-author the *Exploring Heavenly Places* series, which is all about observations from an elevated heavenly perspective!

Another repeating dream was blamed on my dad for many years because he would tell us kids snake stories from his own experiences growing up on a farm in Arkansas. So, for as long as I can remember I've hated those sly, slippery, slithery reptiles. I can't even stand to watch when they pop up on TV, quickly covering my eyes until their screen time is over. With that in mind, it's easy to understand why another recurring prophetic dream from childhood wasn't anything like the pleasant sensation of floating around in the sky. Instead, I would often find myself climbing up on a table or other piece of furniture if inside, or looking for a safe place to stand if outside, because multitudes of snakes were creepy crawling all over the ground. In January 2005, those dreams began to change after I came to Aslan's Place and began experiencing generational deliverance. The more deliverance that was received, the fewer such dreams occurred, because the snakes represented generational issues that needed to be resolved. Thankfully, such night parables are now few and far between and when they do occur they are usually for the purpose of intercession or ministry on someone else's behalf.

Practical Application:

Record any recurring dreams that you've had and do not yet understand.

[1] Genesis 41

CHAPTER NINE
DO THE RESEARCH

Remember having to write research papers in school? There was a time when I hated such assignments, mostly because my researching skills left much to be desired. Procrastination didn't help either, because in those days a delayed trip to the school library to search out relevant information would result in little, if anything, left available for check out. Of course I'm dating myself, because the vast online resources available today make such a concept unimaginable to younger people; but the quantity of results in any web search poses a completely opposite problem—information overload. Just type 'dream interpretation' into any search engine and you will have instant access to millions of documents through which to sift.

Eventually I learned that a research paper is very similar to putting together a jigsaw puzzle. The assignment, as defined by an instructor, would be the equivalent of what the picture on the box should look like when a puzzle is completed. The tidbits of information from here, there, and everywhere would represent the puzzle pieces that eventually fit together to create a coherent image. Dreams are like those research papers, and we should use a multitude of resources to interpret what they mean; and if you're like me and love puzzles, all the better!

A dream seminar I attended early in my quest to understand Dreamspeak taught that an individual should pick just one method and stick with it, preferably purchasing the provider's resources of course. Bad advice! As mentioned before, there is no one-size-fits-all method to understand exactly what God is saying every single time. That said; there are some great places to start, and then remain open to the multitude of ways that the Lord may use to help you comprehend His messages. Remember:

> *It is the glory of God to conceal things, but the glory of kings is to search things out.*[1]

Where to begin? Only one place makes sense—with God. He is the giver of dreams, and He is the ultimate interpreter. Remember Joseph's encounter with the king's cupbearer and baker when he was in prison?

> *They said to him, "We have had dreams, and there is no one to interpret them." And Joseph said to them, "Do not interpretations belong to God?"* [2]

Sometimes, as He did in many biblical examples, God grants an immediate understanding of a dream, but don't forget that 'nothing is always'. It seems fitting that our ultimate teacher is the Holy Spirit because an accurate understanding of Dreamspeak always requires His guidance. When comprehension is not immediate, we can trust Him to lead us to various resources that will help us understand His night parables.

> *But the Helper, the Holy Spirit, whom the Father will send in my name, he will teach you all things and bring to your remembrance all that I have said to you.* [3]

Symbology, or the art of expression by symbols,[4] is an integral tool in our research kit. However, it is vital to use a biblical basis to determine meanings. There are a multitude of dream dictionaries in print and online that provide canned meanings of words, numbers, colors, themes, etc.; but unfortunately many use a frame of reference that is completely based on human understanding and/or allude to philosophical or New Age principles rather than biblical ones. As in every other aspect of life, our best source of guidance is the Bible, which provides precedent for much of what we see in dreams and visions. For example, the principle of repetition:

> *And the doubling of Pharaoh's dream means that the thing is fixed by God, and God will shortly bring it about.* [5]

An immediate sense of understanding is often an important clue in unraveling a larger meaning. Just this morning I awoke and wrote down a dream filled with potentially confusing symbols, but understood how to make sense of them because there was an inner knowledge of the overall context of who and what the dream was about, even though it would not have been immediately apparent to someone else.

Consider how everyday happenings may play into a dream. In the following chapter, I'll illustrate God's creative genius of combining personal experiences and Dreamspeak.

As in any good research paper, an attempt to understand the message of a dream or vision should address the five Ws of grammar—who, what, where, when and why. A few possible queries might include:

- **Who** is the dream about; who are the characters; whom do they represent?
- **What** are they doing; what else is happening; what do things or actions represent?
- **Where** is the setting?
- **When** does it take place (present, past, future/time of day)?
- **Why** would God be showing me this dream?

Practical Application:
Take the who/what/where/when/why queries about your dreams to the Lord before diving into other resources. If there is no clear response, pray for His direction as you begin your research.

[1] Proverbs 25:2

[2] Genesis 40:8

[3] John 14:26

[4] https://www.merriam-webster.com/dictionary/symbology

[5] Genesis 41:32

CHAPTER TEN
WISE COUNSEL

My son recently told me that he understands for the first time how fortunate he's been in his career to have not just one, but two, wonderful mentors. He met the first man during a college internship, and this man not only provided invaluable advice and direction but also helped him procure employment after graduation. They were able to work together at the same company for some time, and were blessed to develop a lasting friendship. Years went by and circumstances had changed for both of them when my son and his wife moved a long distance away, where he got the job of his dreams at just twenty-eight years old. His new boss took an interest in him and things were great for another six years or so until his company was sold to a much larger corporation. Unfortunately, the work environment underwent many changes, one of which was that his boss/mentor/friend eventually resigned to take a job elsewhere. Three bosses later, my son lamented the loss of his mentors, two good friends who had counseled and encouraged him in his career, validating a scriptural truth:

> *Where there is no guidance, a people falls, but in an abundance of counselors there is safety.*[1]

As we've seen, our best teacher is the Holy Spirit, which makes Him our ideal mentor in regard to Dreamspeak. He's the Person we go to first with our dreams, but amazingly enough God loves to let us assist and often enlists other Christians as interpreters. The concept of the Church being a body in which each part, or person, plays an important role in meeting the needs of others is a well established fact[2] so when all else fails, consider asking a trusted friend or adviser for help.

> *Without counsel plans fail, but with many advisers they succeed. To make an apt answer is a joy to a man, and a word in season, how good it is!*[3]

It's common knowledge that people do not think the same way. In general, left-brain thinkers tend toward a logical and analytical thought, while right brainers are more creative or imaginative and tend to think out of the box. There are many other variables as well, such as verbal-versus-visual information processing or integrated life experiences. While anyone can learn to understand dreams, it seems evident that it will be easier for some than for others simply because of the way God wired their brains; and to become proficient it usually takes the teaching and/or counsel of others as well as lots of practice. This is evident in regard to Daniel and his friends—all were very gifted, but only Daniel was a Dreamspeak expert:

> *And the chief of the eunuchs gave them names: Daniel he called Belteshazzar, Hananiah he called Shadrach, Mishael he called Meshach, and Azariah he called Abednego…As for these four youths, God gave them learning and skill in all literature and wisdom, and Daniel had understanding in all visions and dreams.*[4]

Where does one find such counsel? A wide variety of people and resources are available. As mentioned before, my own shelves are loaded down with books, many of which I use regularly as references. Additionally, there may be online sites, in-person seminars, and one-on-one mentoring, to name just a few.

There are times when even the most gifted interpreter may not fully comprehend a dream, in which case wisdom dictates seeking out the insights of mature believers who can help gain understanding. The dreams I get stuck on the most are usually my own, perhaps because I'm too close to 'see the forest through the trees', so to speak. When that happens, I have a couple of trusted friends to help me figure out what I'm missing:

> *…for by wise guidance you can wage your war, and in abundance of counselors there is victory.*[5]

Other times, a dream may be meant to be unraveled within a community of believers. For example, when I first began going to the ministry schools at Aslan's Place I would frequently have a dream the night before that seemed totally indecipherable, but as the day would proceed and events unfolded, it would turn out I'd been given part of the agenda for the day in advance. Outside of those sessions my dreams had no relevance, for God's intent was for them to be deciphered as a group. This often happens with others as well, and it's not uncommon that the first thing Paul says to me when I walk into a gathering is, "Did you get the dream I sent you this morning?" Then his dream becomes the blueprint for new revelation that God wants to deliver to all of us.

Practical Application:

Begin to identify the resources for your own 'research library'. That God should be first on the list is a given; but next, identify printed materials, online helps, audio-visual presentations, seminars, and think about what people you know who can assist you in the quest to interpret your dreams. Ask the Lord to guide you to the resources that are best for you.

[1] Proverbs 11:14

[2] 1 Corinthians 12

[3] Proverbs 15:22-23

[4] Daniel 1:1, 17

[5] Proverbs 24:6

Chapter Eleven
TWILIGHT TIME

Initially released in 1944, the song, *Twilight Time*, has been recorded by well over fifty artists. Most notable is the #1 hit from 1958, with the Platters crooning lyrical reflections of romance amidst the brilliant and seemingly magical moments of sunset.[1] More recently *Twilight* (a novel) and *The Twilight Saga* (a film series), portray the dangerous romance of a teenage girl who falls in love with a vampire. And who can forget the psychological and supernatural horror of Rod Serling's TV series, the black-and-white-but-enduring *Twilight Zone*? It seems clear that twilight has a mystique all its own.

While twilight may represent either dusk or dawn when the sun meets the horizon, it can also refer to an intermediate state in which things are not clearly defined.[2] As it relates to Dreamspeak, the term best represents the moments between sleep and wakefulness, the time when the dreamer is in transition between the spiritual and natural realms. It's an unusual time when information from both sides of our consciousness can be processed and understood concurrently; a time when we may discern very clearly the messages God is sharing. Consider Job 12:22 (NLT):

> *He uncovers mysteries hidden in darkness; he brings light to the deepest gloom.*

Albert Barnes, a theologian during the 1800s further illustrated Job's comment:

> God discloses truths which are wholly beyond the power of man to discover - truths that seem to be hidden in profound night. This may refer either to the revelation which God was believed to have furnished, or to his power of bringing out the most secret thoughts and purposes, or to his power of predicting future events by bringing them out of darkness to the clear light of day, or

> to his power of detecting plots, intrigues, and conspiracies.[3]

My friend, Jana Green, is both a gifted seer and an amazing artist. She shared her insight into the importance of twilight experiences:

> Twilight is that place between awake and asleep, the meditative state in which we are connected to the heart with a sub-conscious un-awareness. Upon waking, the things that come to the surface are often the beliefs of the heart, which I realize we can choose to keep or send away.
>
> For the most part, meditation has long been all but ignored in the western church, but this is a meditative place were we can return and re-create beliefs to line up with truth. As a little child, I would imagine all sorts of creative things and I believed them. Unfortunately, as we get older, we leave this delta place of feeling to conform more to our environment and leave the creative realm behind. But what if we could return to this restful state? What if we were not so affected by our circumstances? I believe the heart could re-instate the original intent for it is eternity that was written in our hearts.[4] After all, the Creator Himself fearfully and wonderfully made us,[5] and through this intentional meditation on the things of God we can change our lives and all that is around us so that creation itself may be redeemed from its depravity.[6]
>
> It is in the twilight that I experience remembrance of the Lord in my life long before I knew him, and believe this is where the Holy Spirit can remind us of all things past, present, and future.

Interesting concept, huh? The Holy Spirit can 'remind' us of things we couldn't possibly be aware of in the now. He was there when our spirits were created long before conception; He watched our formation in the womb; He witnessed every historical event from before the foundation of the world; He knew each of our ancestors intimately; and His already-existent presence in the future not only supplied the rich biblical prophecies but also enable Him to share with His prophetic people what is yet to come.

> *I am the Alpha and the Omega," says the Lord God, "who is and who was and who is to come, the Almighty.*[7]

Speaking of Jana, she was the subject of one of the most incredible twilight experiences of my life. In 2008, we were roommates at a Hilton Hotel in London, England while attending an Aslan's Place school of ministry. A comparable room in the USA would have had two double or queen sized beds, separated by at least several feet, and plenty of room to navigate on either side. Not so in London, where hotel rooms appear to have been shrunk to about half size. Our twin beds were placed right next to each other, the mattresses only about two inches apart and very little space on the sides. Unfortunately, we weren't the most ideal roommates! On the one hand, she slept much less than me and kept the light on at all hours; but on the other, when she did try to sleep my snoring kept her awake. On this night though, we were of one accord. Both went to bed at the same time and while she fell fast asleep, I entered a twilight kind of rest in which I was having a very direct spirit-to-Spirit conversation with the Lord; yet I knew exactly where we were and that Jana was asleep right beside me. I was astonished as I prayed for her, "Lord, please give Jana peace," and she would sigh, "Ahhhh." "Lord, please help Jana to rest." "Ohhhh." On this went for what seemed like several minutes as God directly administered every request, and she responded with sighs of absolute contentment.

> *Praise the Lord! Blessed is the man who fears the Lord, who greatly delights in his commandments...Light dawns in the darkness for the upright; he is gracious, merciful, and righteous.*[8]

On another twilight occasion in 2006, a special message dawned for me as I struggled in my battle against breast cancer:

> It was very clear in my mind as I awoke this morning, "Life itself is a risk; life requires faith; importance or value is not determined by appearance." Pretty significant and

> encouraging thoughts in light of the fact that I am in the midst of chemotherapy and I'm completely bald. Every day is a struggle to keep on trusting God.

In other twilight moments, I've heard words of knowledge, seen quick visions, received instructions, gained flashes of insight into the meaning of dreams, and on and on. Needless to say, it's very important to pay attention to these transitional moments of clarity between dimensions.

Practical Application:

Pay careful attention to moments between sleep and wakefulness, and make a note of anything heard, seen or sensed. Later, when fully awake, ponder and pray into the twilight experience to fully grasp the meaning of what God was communicating.

[1] https://en.wikipedia.org/wiki/Twilight_Time_(song)

[2] https://www.merriam-webster.com/dictionary/twilight

[3] http://biblehub.com/commentaries/job/12-22.htm

[4] Ecclesiastes 3:11

[5] Psalm 139:14

[6] Romans 8:21

[7] Revelation 1:8

[8] Psalm 112:1, 4

CHAPTER TWELVE
A GOD'S EYE VIEW

Scripture is quite clear that God's knowledge is much greater than ours and His ways are beyond finding out. Not confined by the time or space that He created, I AM, our eternal God, is omniscient; He is all knowing:

> *Before the mountains were brought forth, or ever you had formed the earth and the world, from everlasting to everlasting you are God.*[1]

> *Have you not known? Have you not heard? The Lord is the everlasting God, the Creator of the ends of the earth. He does not faint or grow weary; his understanding is unsearchable.*[2]

> *For my thoughts are not your thoughts, neither are your ways my ways, declares the LORD.*[3]

God's omnipotence is well illustrated in Psalm 2, where we see that even the nations of the world are subject to His power as He sits in the heavens and laughs at the foolish plots of evil mankind. Time and again, the Lord's power is evident throughout scripture, so much so that we have already written two volumes in this series about it, yet have barely scratched the surface.[4]

In Psalm 139, David beautifully declares the majestic, incomparable omnipresence of God:

> *Where shall I go from your Spirit?*
> *Or where shall I flee from your presence?*
> *If I ascend to heaven, you are there!*
> *If I make my bed in Sheol, you are there!*
> *If I take the wings of the morning and dwell in the uttermost parts of the sea, even there your hand shall lead me, and your right hand shall hold me.*
> *If I say, "Surely the darkness shall cover me, and the light about me be night," even the darkness is not dark to you; the night is bright as the day, for darkness is as light with you.*[5]

There can be no question that God has a unique view of all that was, is, and is to come; nothing is hidden from Him—ever! Amazingly enough, this omniscient, omnipotent, omnipresent God loves to share His wisdom and knowledge with us, a concept that is integral to *Exploring Heavenly Places.* How important it is that we remember the truth of our position with Him, an exalted seat from which He allows us glimpses of our world through His eyes.

> *But God, being rich in mercy, because of the great love with which he loved us, even when we were dead in our trespasses, made us alive together with Christ—by grace you have been saved—and raised us up with him and seated us with him in the heavenly places in Christ Jesus* [6]

What a vantage point! It is the lookout spot from which we are allowed to see things the way God sees them; it is a panoramic view to marvel at; it is a change of focus through which we can be informed, comforted, healed, and delivered as we trust in the Lord and do not lean on our own understanding;[7] it is the outlook that is available from our dreams.

On February 5, 2017, the Elijah List published an article by Edie Bayer of Houston, Texas; *God is Calling Us Higher – to Get His Perspective!* She shared a wonderful vision in which the Lord showed her how things appear to Him.[8] Reading it, I was thrilled because I had just had a similar experience in a dream the day before. In an email to Paul I wrote:

> Good word! It validates a recent dream that I knew right away was a God's eye view. I was watching as a book was being written, and knew it was in the heavenly library and was an unchangeable record. I saw that toward the front of the book some of the text was in red, like in a red-letter Bible, and I understood that Jesus himself had written in this book. In tandem it seems, I also saw a baby with a very full diaper. Later, I was the private duty nurse for a woman in a hospital bed who was very peaceful and relaxed following her treatment, which hadn't been pretty because it was a bowel obstruction that had to be

> manually cleared out (not a pleasant task for either the medical personnel or the patient, I can assure you!). When I woke up I knew that this was God's perspective of our government and our nation. The baby represented the new Trump administration and woman represented the nation. Both initially appeared very messy and definitely needed cleansing, but the ultimate result was cleanliness (representing righteousness) and total peace and rest (as opposed to what we see in news reports these days).

Even as I write this chapter I remain excited, for my prayer from the beginning of this project has been to receive God's inspiration regarding the things He wants to say about dreams, and though I'd recorded and shared my dream, I hadn't stopped to think it might be part of this book until I began writing. Thanks be to Him for using someone else's vision to remind me of an important message about Dreamspeak—when we dream we have a front row seat—a God's eye view!

Practical Application:

Ask the Lord to reveal His view of what you see in your dreams and study scriptures that illustrate His omniscience, omnipotence, and omnipresence. Ask Him to show you how your dreams express His perspective. Thank Him for confirmations and instruction that comes through others.

[1] Psalm 90:2

[2] Isaiah 40:28

[3] Isaiah 55:8

[4] *Exploring Heavenly Places, Volume 4, Power in the Heavenly Places;* and *Volume 5, The Power of God, on Earth as it is in Heaven*

[5] Psalm 139:7-12

[6] Ephesians 2:4-6

[7] Proverbs 3:5

[8]http://www.elijahlist.com/words/display_word.html?ID=17427

CHAPTER THIRTEEN
WHY, AND WHAT-IF?

Have you ever experienced the sweet exasperation of trying to satisfy the curiosity of a toddler who endlessly asks, "Why?" No matter your response there's always another, "But why?" Perhaps, like me, you've reached the point on occasion when you finally answered with an exasperated, "Because I said so, that's why!"

Sometimes our queries about dreams can seem just as unanswerable. We know our understanding must come only from a biblical basis, but what if there is no one verse that seems to address a particular question? Why, why, why? This is when we have to learn to live by faith and simply trust God; this is where we can hold onto biblical principles that we cherish but have probably never even considered in terms of dreams.

> *All Scripture is breathed out by God and profitable for teaching, for reproof, for correction, and for training in righteousness, that the man of God may be complete, equipped for every good work.*[1]

At the risk of repeating myself—well, OK, I definitely am repeating myself, but this is important! All dream interpretations belong to God and we must seek His perspective. We simply cannot make assumptions based on our own understanding, or lack of, without talking to Him about it. He does satisfy our longings, and while He may not provide a direct answer, He will lead us to a biblically based 'ah-ha' moment:

> *Do not be anxious about anything, but in everything by prayer and supplication with thanksgiving let your requests be made known to God. And the peace of God, which surpasses all understanding, will guard your hearts and your minds in Christ Jesus.*[2]

A friend asked me recently if we could sin in our dreams, after finding himself sleeping with women other than his wife in his dreams. Hmmmm...now that you mention it, I've had dreams in which I did things I'd never, ever, consider either! So why do we forge ahead in our dreams with such flagrant disregard to God's righteous standards? There could be a multitude of reasons, ranging from secret-and-sinful desires of the heart that we may not consciously realize, to false dreams from the enemy in an attempt to make us feel guilt or shame, to generational sin that leaves us vulnerable, to any number of other possibilities. In every case, the solution remains the same—take it to the Lord in prayer and find out what He wants to do about it. If convicted of a secret sin or a generational issue, repent and receive His forgiveness, which is always freely given. If it's the enemy, what's the big deal? God is still bigger, so ask Him to deal with it and choose to trust Him; or if it's an obvious lie, simply dismiss it and send deception packing in Jesus' name. God always has a solution! Remember:

> *I lay down and slept; I woke again, for the Lord sustained me. I will not be afraid of many thousands of people who have set themselves against me all around.*[3]

> *In peace I will both lie down and sleep; for you alone, O Lord, make me dwell in safety.*[4]

This is a truth that God proved to me in no uncertain terms! One night I had a sense of terrible evil beside my bed and I knew I was in danger, but I was so exhausted and weak from a recent surgery that I couldn't deal with it. The best I could manage was to remind the Lord of the verses above and ask Him to have my back before I conked out. Throughout the night there was one scene after another of a two evil characters, one male and one female, who befriended their victims, wooed them into illicit sexual situations, and then murdered them. Amazingly, even though they seemed to know they would die, they happily and blindly went along with them as willing participants in their destruction, so reminiscent of King Solomon's words to his son:

> *With much seductive speech she persuades him; with her smooth talk she compels him All at once he follows her, as an ox goes to the slaughter, or as a stag is caught fast till an arrow pierces its liver; as a bird rushes into a snare; he does not know that it will cost him his life.*[5]

Finally, the male figure got around to me, and now he appeared as an ugly, misshapen, horrible spirit whose influence was mesmerizing. Just as I was about to succumb, and at the very moment of his attempt to rape, a man who I knew was the Lord appeared and lopped off his head. I awoke shaken to my core, with the certain knowledge of two things: first, I really had been physically attacked by an evil entity; and second, without a doubt, God had my back and Jesus had delivered me from a serious evil attempt against my life. Interestingly enough, this happened while we were in the process of researching the fallen sons of God, and when I talked to Paul about it, he discerned that the bad guy in my dream was one of those fallen sons. Perhaps you recall that these are the same unrighteous beings that mated with the daughters of men, producing offspring who were the Nephilim.[6] The important point here is that no matter what evil comes against you in a dream, God is always sufficient to overcome it.

More questions…but, but, but…I still feel absolutely terrible when I wake up! How could I have done such a thing? Oh me, oh my, what have I done? I feel so guilty! Oh, woe is me!

Perhaps a seemingly willful sin or error in a dream for which we simply don't have satisfactory resolution would be a good scenario for learning to rest in the truth of God's word. Consider the apostle Paul's victorious proclamation right after he's spent a whole chapter moaning about his own why-in-the-world-did-I-do-that questions:

> *There is therefore now no condemnation for those who are in Christ Jesus. For the law of the Spirit of life has set you free in Christ Jesus from the law of sin and death.*[7]

Or, how about this one: what if the dream is nightmarish, so frightening, that I awake in a cold sweat, shaking with fear? What if it's a terrifying nightmare? Daniel could relate; his dreams and visions were so intense that he literally became ill:

> *And I, Daniel, was overcome and lay sick for some days. Then I rose and went about the king's business, but I was appalled by the vision and did not understand it.*[8]

Fortunately, Daniel was intimately acquainted with the One from Whom his strength came, and he understood to take such matters of concern to the God he trusted with all his heart:

> *Then I turned my face to the Lord God, seeking him by prayer and pleas for mercy with fasting and sackcloth and ashes. I prayed to the Lord my God…*[9]

The answer for us today remains the same; take it to the Lord in prayer. He knows our thoughts and fears even before we do, so nobody is better qualified to help:

> *Even before a word is on my tongue, behold, O Lord, you know it altogether.*[10]

Recently, after a long, busy day I was more than ready to sleep but it just wouldn't come. Was it because I was visiting a friend and trying to sleep in a new place? Was it intercession for the seminar at Aslan's Place the following day? Was there something God wanted me to know? After several hours of tossing and turning, asking why and complaining to the Lord, I finally fell asleep, only to awaken with a start after a very short time, almost paralyzed in shock from a frightening dream. How could that be? What did that mean?

> I had been in my house, which didn't look at all like reality, and my sister showed up (no matter that she lives in New Mexico and I am in California). Then my aunt and uncle arrived, and I was calling my mom to let her know they were there. (Hmmm, another logistical problem here—my mom and uncle have both been in Heaven for several years, and my aunt is hundreds of miles away) Meanwhile, as I looked around there was a table full of junk that needed to be cleaned up. Then I heard the loud noise of a helicopter directly overhead and was astounded to see that it was hovering right outside my window. As I wondered aloud why it was so close, each of my relatives yelled, "I'm out of here," and disappeared, as if vaporized; leaving me laid out flat on the floor and staring up at the ceiling in a daze because I had just experienced a blast

> that could only be described as atomic. Weirdly enough, there was no visible damage from the impact to my house, which represents my life.

Ohhh, I was sooo tired! I pleaded, "Lord, why would I have a dream like this? I need sleep, and this is what I get? What is going on?" Fortunately, I was rational enough to realize that the helicopter had been white, indicating a righteous mission, so I tiredly told Him I was leaving it with Him and sure hoped He'd help me figure it out in the morning, turned over, and quickly fell back asleep. But the night was not to be restful, and five or six more dreams occurred, with me waking briefly between each one, full of why questions but not alert enough to write then down. Finally, I woke up at 4 AM, with a subtle knowledge that the ongoing dreams had been about my friend's home, and each one of them had been progressively better. You see, just before bed, she had asked me to pray over her property because she was aware of evil that she'd been unable to get rid of. Even so, it was still the middle of the night and I was very interested in sleeping, but it wasn't to be so I reluctantly gave up and got up to pray and journal until finally just before dawn, I crept as quietly as possible into the kitchen for a much needed cup of coffee. Everything had changed! An unidentified righteous being that I suspected might be a power was standing in the kitchen doorway and I discerned healing in the kitchen. Checking things out, I discovered another being at a sliding window to the patio and one at the front door that felt like it could be one of several possibilities but I couldn't discern which one. (Hours later at the Aslan's Place seminar, the Lord revealed Wisdom and ushered us through a gate into her house, at which point I realized it was Wisdom that had been standing at my friend's door!) Only when my friend finally awoke from a very peaceful and restful night did I come to understand the earth shattering first dream more fully, for as I shared it, her expression became more and more bemused. As it turned out, my relatives represented people in her own family: a sister, aunt, uncle, and mother, all of whom are dead. Yet, there had still been unrighteous connections enabling the evil she'd been discerning in her home. My sleepless night had now become a gift because I realized I had not only witnessed the awesome 'atomic' power of God to annihilate His enemies, but had also been blessed by my friend's joy that her home was now spiritually clean.

Practical Application:

Consider the difficult questions you may have about dreams and then search out biblical principles that may apply to them.

[1] 2 Timothy 3:16-17
[2] Philippians 4:6-7
[3] Psalm 3:5-6
[4] Psalm 4:8
[5] Proverbs 7:21-23
[6] Genesis 6
[7] Romans 8:1
[8] Daniel 8:37
[9] Daniel 9:3-4a
[10] Psalm 139:4

CHAPTER FOURTEEN
INTENTIONALITY

Can we intentionally alter our dreams, taking action to change outcomes? This is another directly unanswerable question if we're looking for an exact Bible quote, but one that can be resolved indirectly. Scripture is clear that we are to be conformed to the image of Christ,[1] and that we must:

> *...work out your own salvation with fear and trembling, for it is God who works in you, both to will and to work for his good pleasure.*[2]

As mentioned before, my sleep used to be plagued by snakes, but as I began receiving generational prayer at Aslan's Place those night parables rapidly receded. It seems clear that the intentional action of pursuing deliverance resulted in becoming more conformed to Jesus' image and produced a dramatic change in my dreams.

It would also appear that the more we mature in Him, the more both the significance and understanding of our dreams increases. It's not uncommon for unbelievers to have one short dream that they just can't get out of their mind—something they've never come close to understanding—and when a Christian interprets it, they are astounded and the Lord opens wide their hearts to receive whatever God is telling them. Some Christians routinely do evangelism outreaches, offering to interpret dreams and the responses are usually overwhelmingly positive. In fact, it often seems that non-Christians are much more receptive than many long-time Christians who have become conformed to fundamentalist doctrines that declare that God no longer speaks in dreams and visions. They live in fear that to consider dream interpretation is dangerous because one might be lured into New Age thought and practice.

I often work with individuals who are seeking to understand their dreams, and most initially began with significant deliverance dreams. Once those issues are addressed and healing is received, the dreams usually transition as to become more about comfort, encouragement, or guidance. Often, prophetic dreams may enter the picture as well.

False dreams may occur too, and can be realized as such simply because a false doctrine that skews a biblical truth is recognized. Satan is clearly presented as an outright liar throughout scripture,[3] so we must know what the Bible actually says and not just what someone has told us it says in order to keep from being deceived in a dream. We may awake unsure or even distressed about a dream but when things don't line up with what is known to be true, it can usually be dismissed as false. Alternatively, as one becomes more skilled in discernment they may be able to ask the Lord and then physically discern whether it is good or evil. A memorable false dream for me happened shortly after I entered into a level of relationship with God that I knew exactly who I am in Christ Jesus. But in my dream my purse went missing and I couldn't find it. As soon a awoke I realized immediately that the purse represented my identity and the enemy had tried to steal it; so instead of obsessing over why this happened, I quickly and easily discarded it and asked the Lord to deal with the deceiver on my behalf.

Years ago when Hal Lindsay's *Late, Great Planet Earth* was first released, there was a huge shift in focus among my Christian friends toward the idea of the Rapture. We thought about it, talked about it, and listened to sermons about it endlessly—it was definitely the hot topic of the day! I also began having frequent Rapture dreams in which there would be a 'suddenly moment' when there was an awareness that Jesus was coming back and I would begin rising up in the air along with many others. But such dreams always ended quickly because each time I would recall scriptural facts that were distorted and then wake up. May we all be able to declare:

> *Your statutes have been my songs in the house of my sojourning. I remember your name in the night, O Lord, and keep your law.*[4]

That the current spiritual condition of one's heart is relevant in dreams is evident in the life of King Solomon:

> *At Gibeon the Lord appeared to Solomon in a dream by night, and God said, "Ask what I shall give you." And Solomon said, "You have shown great and steadfast love to your servant David my father, because he walked before you in faithfulness, in righteousness, and in uprightness of heart toward you. And you have kept for him this great and steadfast love and have given him a son to sit on his throne this day…Give your servant therefore an understanding mind to govern your people, that I may discern between good and evil, for who is able to govern this your great people?" It pleased the Lord that Solomon had asked this…And Solomon awoke, and behold, it was a dream.*[5]

It seems very clear that the more we hide the Word of God in our hearts[6] and seek an intimate relationship with Him, the less likely we are to be led astray by false dreams.

Sadly, it's also clear from the life of King Saul that sin and outright disobedience to God can result in an absence of dreams:

> *And when Saul inquired of the Lord, the Lord did not answer him, either by dreams, or by Urim, or by prophets…Then Samuel said to Saul, "Why have you disturbed me by bringing me up?" Saul answered, "I am in great distress, for the Philistines are warring against me, and God has turned away from me and answers me no more, either by prophets or by dreams. Therefore I have summoned you to tell me what I shall do."* [7]

God sent Samuel to anoint David as king over Israel, but as great a king as he became, he was a man after God's own heart.[8] Israel soon began turning to idolatry after David's death and it was only a little over two hundred years before Isaiah was prophesying:

> *For the Lord has poured out upon you a spirit of deep sleep, and has closed your eyes (the prophets), and covered your heads (the seers). And the vision of all this has become to you like the words of a book that is sealed. When men give it to one who can read, saying, "Read this," he says, "I cannot, for it is sealed." And when they give the book to one who cannot read, saying, "Read this," he says, "I cannot read."* [9]

There can be no question that our intentional actions can affect not only the quantity but also the quality of dreams and visions in our lives. Also, like so many other wonderful gifts from the Lord they may have become blocked for a variety of reasons, including generational sins, curses, ungodly proclamations, etc. Appendix 1 offers a prayer to deal with such issues and release dreams.

Practical Application:

Continue to pursue intimacy with God, learning to recognize His voice. Pursue your own healing through deliverance, personal payer and Bible study so that the improving condition of your heart will be reflected in your dreams, and so you cannot be easily deceived.

[1] Romans 8:29

[2] Philippians 2:12b-13

[3] Genesis 3:4; John 8:44,

[4] Psalm 119:54-55

[5] 1 Kings 3:5-6, 9-10, 15

[6] Psalm 119:11

[7] 1 Samuel 28:6,15

[8] 1 Samuel 13:14

[9] Isaiah 29:10-12

CHAPTER FIFTEEN
DISCERNMENT

Anyone who's been around the ministry of Paul Cox and Aslan's Place for more than a few minutes has heard about the importance of understanding discernment so we can follow Jesus' example of doing only what the Father is doing. But, what do discernment and dreams have to do with one another? Lots!

> *But solid food is for the mature, for those who have their powers of discernment trained by constant practice to distinguish good from evil.*[1]

We've explored the dimensional quality of dreams; we've examined the concept of seeing things from God's eye view; we've seen scripture after scripture that validates God's practice of communicating through dreams. It's clear that discernment is also biblical, but how do dreams and discernment operate together?

Rob Gross is the pastor of Mountain View Community Church in Kaneohe, Hawaii, and his discernment is very similar to Paul's. He is known not only for teaching the principles of discernment but also for leading his church to put them into practice, as is well documented in his book about the healing miracles they have witnessed, *Exploring Heavenly Places, Volume 6: Miracles on the Mountain of the Lord.* Rob is also a dreamer, and a couple of his dreams illustrate well the practical relationship between discernment and dreams.

> I met Dr. Paul Cox in 2001, in Hawaii. He prayed for me, and the next day I began to discern the heavenly realms. In 1997, I had received a prophetic word that I would receive the gift of discernment. Reflecting back, I was already discerning things before Paul prayed for me but was not aware that it was discernment.
>
> On an early Sunday morning in 1998, I was dreaming that I was floating in space. Hovering above the earth, I felt a

> large hand come and grab me between my left bicep and forearm. As this was happening, the word 'suicide' came into my spirit.
>
> Several hours later, I was about to stand up to speak at church when I felt the same sensation that I had experienced in the dream. Wanting to see if the Lord was up to something, I asked the congregation, "Is there anyone here who has either attempted suicide recently or is thinking of ending their life now?" As I looked out into the congregation, a man sitting to my left in the back of our facility raised his hand. Instead of airing out his laundry in front of everyone, I asked him to see me after the service.
>
> Later, this man who was in his late twenties, shared with me that he had tried to hang himself with his belt because his marriage was breaking apart. The belt snapped and his attempt failed. I listened intently, hugged and encouraged him to trust God, and prayed for the Lord to intervene in his life. Now, many years later, this man is well and alive. Hallelujah!

In February 2017, Paul had finished a very difficult phone ministry session in which terrible depths of evil had been encountered, and he was so physically and emotionally wrung out that he could barely function. That night Rob dreamed:

> Paul, 5 or 6 other believers, and I were sitting around a table in a class on the 2nd floor of Shirokiya, the White Tree Store at Ala Moana Shopping Center in Honolulu. Paul was conducting a class when I felt dizzy and nauseous and lay down on the floor. Lying there, I discerned a tree branch on my right foot and got up to tell Paul about it. Not to my surprise, he had already drawn a picture of a tree branch on a piece of paper and was already explaining it to those around the table.
>
> In the second and final scene, Paul was not well and

> slumped onto the floor up against a wall. He told me that whatever he was dealing with had something to do with the dimensions and asked me to pray for him. I obliged, and knelt down beside him and prayed.

Rob noted that his dizzy, nauseous sensation within the dream was reminiscent of Isaiah's words:

> *The Lord has poured into them a spirit of dizziness; they make Egypt stagger in all that she does, as a drunkard staggers around in his vomit.*[2]

Once Rob awoke, he texted the dream to Paul, adding that he could hear a low frequency humming sound, which he identified as the dimensions. Later, they also spoke on the phone and as Rob prayed for Paul, he disconnected him from any ungodly branches, windows, doors, gates and corridors in the dimensions.[3] Paul immediately felt the deliverance, and speaking to me later in the day, he shared how much better he felt after the prayer.

Consider the intricate tapestry of dreams and discernment that God wove together to equip Rob to assist Him in delivering healing to two of His kids. In the first example, God knew all about the suicide attempt of the young man and He also knew that the man would be in church that morning. So God delivered the physical discernment within a dream to Rob, then a word of knowledge, and finally He repeated the sensation just as Rob was about to speak; ultimately allowing this pastor, through his own attention and obedience, to minister to the suffering man.

In the second case, having experienced a discernment dream in which he had both felt Paul's suffering and observed the spiritual causes behind it, Rob was equipped to pray effectively for him. A couple of things are interesting here in addition to Rob's obedience: Paul was separated by thousands of miles and 3 time zones from his client on the east, and from Rob on the west; but from God's vantage point He could see it all. I believe that Rob was actually ministering to Paul in the dream and that his prayer helped until such time as they could be on the phone together to resolve the issue more completely.

Only God! No one on earth could ever have seen the needs and delivered the solutions through multiple dimensions of time and space, and through both the physical and spiritual realities, but God used Rob to deliver healing for both the young man and Paul.

> *Then he said to me, "This is the word of the LORD to Zerubbabel: Not by might, nor by power, but by my Spirit, says the LORD of hosts.*[4]

There can be no doubt that God is not dimensionally limited. There can be no doubt that God sees and knows all that concerns His people (and everyone else, for that matter!). And, there can certainly be no doubt that He uses of all of the means at His disposal to communicate with those who love Him and who are on alert for His instruction so they can co-operate with what the Father is doing.

Practical Application:

Pay attention to physical sensations within dreams and consider what that discernment could mean and how God wants you to use it to do what the Father is doing.

[1] Hebrews 5:14

[2] Isaiah 19:14 (NIV)

[3] A wealth of information about these things can be accessed by using the search function at http://aslansplace.com/language/en/about-aslans-place/

[4] Zechariah 4:6

CHAPTER SIXTEEN
DELIVERANCE

During prayer ministry, a dream brought to memory by the Holy Spirit often provides the clues we need to get to the root of an individual's issues and help them experience deliverance and healing. Whether the need is in relation to generational sin or an inner healing issue, it is clear that God often reveals the hurting conditions of the heart in dreams and visions:

> *You have tried my heart, you have visited me by night, you have tested me, and you will find nothing; I have purposed that my mouth will not transgress.*[1]

> *In a dream, in a vision of the night, when deep sleep falls on men, while they slumber on their beds, then he opens the ears of men and terrifies them with warnings, that he may turn man aside from his deed and conceal pride from a man; he keeps back his soul from the pit, his life from perishing by the sword.*[2]

Remember how I explained to the Lord that I was willing to write this book, but would need to rely on Him to give me new insights and inspiration? Imagine my surprise when, in July 2016, He did just that a few days later!

Aslan's Place had referred Sanji to me for help with her dreams, and within seconds of our initial conversation I knew without a doubt that this was a divine appointment. She'd had a series of 6 dreams, so I asked her to email them to me so I could ponder them before we talked again. When they arrived, I instantly knew what they meant, but I also realized that they would have a much greater impact on her life if she heard the interpretation directly from Jesus. So, off we went on an adventure with Him that is ongoing, for my now-dear friend is quite a dreamer!

An abbreviated version of her dreams follows, the first two almost identical:

> Dreams 1 and 2: My friend was using my car, and she crashed it without telling me. The next day, I saw her and asked about my car, having realized I had left my purse in it and needed to retrieve it. Ignoring me, she pretended she did not hear. Unhappy that she did not have respect either for my car or me, I asked her to give it back.
>
> Dream 3: I had gone into the mall to do some errands and could not find my car when I returned to the parking lot. I went back inside a store and then came outside again. This time my car was there.
>
> Dream 4: I was driving a red car in a heavy snowfall and ice was frozen on the road. Some ice was melting, and suddenly I saw my car sliding into a ditch and me pushing it out of the ditch onto the slippery, frozen, icy road, and heading uphill.
>
> Dream 5: I saw myself in a chartered bus and they dropped me off at a place where some people were waiting. Then a helicopter appeared and a woman alighted from the chopper and asked who wanted to go with her.
>
> Dream 6: I was riding in an old, pink, vintage convertible and Jesus was driving the car. The wind was blowing and our hair was flying.

Without going into the much-longer details, meanings, and personal revelation that evolved from Sanji's dreams, the summary is that Jesus walked her step by step through each one, not only showing her the meaning but also administering a tremendous amount of healing along the way. In the first three, a loss of identity and feelings of insecurity, anxiety, and being ignored or disrespected were acknowledged and healed; and she stepped into her true identity in Christ. In dream 4, she learned that life is simply too hard to do everything on her own and invited Jesus to help her. No big surprise, He did! As we prayed through dream 5, Sanji made the choice to get in the helicopter, only to realize that Jesus was the pilot and she could now begin to fly in the Spirit. Finally, dream 6 provided encouraging evidence that Jesus is the one 'driving' her life and that there is a sense of freedom such as she's never known with Him now seated behind the wheel.

Our adventure together has continued. In fact, as I write this, a couple of new dreams that she needs some help with are waiting in an email. Each time we talk is a blessing straight from the heart of our Father because He has knit our hearts together with His love.

Practical Application:

Review your dreams to identify difficult situations in which you find yourself. Ask the Lord to show you what he wants you to know; try to interpret what the symbols mean; if necessary, contact a trusted friend or a prayer minister to help you receive the deliverance that the Lord wants to administer.

[1] Psalm 17:3

[2] Job 33:15-18

CHAPTER SEVENTEEN

A BACKDOOR PRAYER

I often wonder what a life experience would mean if it were a dream, but this time it never even crossed my mind. I'd been really happy with my laptop for more than six years, but now it seemed to be in rapidly declining health; either running excruciatingly slow or freezing in the middle of a task, which required a restart of the affected program(s). Apparently, computer technology ages even more quickly than me, because the old processor just wasn't enough to keep up with the newest operating system. The final straw came when the computer slipped off a stool and hit the floor, resulting in sparkly green pixels showing through on the screen. After a trip to the store to do some research, I configured a new computer and ordered it online, and it arrived a couple weeks later. I busily went to work setting up my new toy, completely forgetting my God-encounters from the previous night.

> *For God speaks in one way, and in two, though man does not perceive it. In a dream, in a vision of the night, when deep sleep falls on men, while they slumber on their beds, then he opens the ears of men and terrifies them with warnings, that he may turn man aside from his deed and conceal pride from a man…*[1]

In a dream, I had been in a restaurant where food was ordered and picked up at a counter, and there were a few tables scattered around. Three unidentified friends (representing Father, Son and Holy Spirit) accompanied me. There was one table for four available, but it was right next to the service line and was very crowded and noisy. One friend suggested we go upstairs where there were some more tables so we headed up the steps. I didn't actually see the room, but knew instinctively that it was surprisingly spacious and open.

At the same time, in one of those inexplicable ways that dreams can multitask, there had been an ongoing experience in which I had received what looked like a balloon with a small amount of water in it, maybe 1/3 full with plenty of room for expansion. I knew this represented my writing and ministry, with the Spirit (water) as both my inspiration and foundation. It's exciting to contemplate what things will look like as I allow Him to 'fill my balloon' and expand my horizons!

When morning arrived, I remembered that much earlier in the night I had been awake briefly and received the word, 'backdoor', with no understanding of what it was about. There was awareness that I had been developing a prayer in my sleep but couldn't remember it. Then I realized that my mind/brain is like an exquisitely designed computer, and that programmers often leave a backdoor entry so they can get in when nobody else can and, hmmm, God is my programmer! I got up, wrote down the dream, wrote a 'backdoor prayer', and asked the Lord to apply to me everything I had written and prayed during the dream state, even though I couldn't recall the exact words:

> Lord, please forgive my generational line and me for all unrighteous thought and for believing the lies of the enemy.[2] Please forgive me for not setting my mind on things above and for allowing fear, worry, and regret to dominate my thinking.[3]
>
> Lord, You are my Creator/Designer/Programmer. Please access Your backdoor to my brain/mind, which is like an elaborate computer system. Close all doors that should be closed, and open all doors that should be opened so the gates of my mind may never be shut against You. Please kill all viruses and erase all ungodly pathways. Please upgrade my speed, memory, and storage capacity so I can quickly process and recall all that You want me to know. Please re-program me; upgrade my existing programs and install new ones that align with your latest designs for my life; and set my entire being for automatic updates and releases. Please build a firewall of Your truth through which deception cannot penetrate, and install the Word of God as my always-up-to-date anti-virus program. Please cause all of my thoughts to be aligned with Yours so I can always understand what You are doing and know

> how to respond appropriately in the world. Conform me to Your image, Lord.

The full extent of how the computer experience in the natural related not only to my dream but also to the experiences of others wasn't realized until two days later. I had received a request from Paul Cox to interpret a dream that he had received from Dawn Bray. [4] Not immediately having an understanding, I'd left it overnight and asked the Lord to show me what it meant. Right after I wrote and prayed the backdoor prayer, I looked at the dream again and all of the pieces immediately fell into place. I sent the interpretation to Paul and Dawn, and before long she responded:

> This made me laugh. I had a dream last night about the back door being unlocked and I was going to check the door (but never did) and then dreamed the same thing a second time (which for me is the Lord highlighting something for sure). It was the end of a dream you interpreted.

No matter how often God does something like this, I will never cease to be astounded by His creativity in revealing things He wants me to know. It's often one puzzle piece at a time through dreams, the Bible, or His still small voice; not to mention the way He tosses in wonderful confirmations from other people, even when they live clear across the county and we haven't been in contact for a long time. In fact, we've never even met in person!

Aslan's Place released the prayer and there was immediate feedback from people who discerned deliverance from it. Recently though, another wonderful testimony came from a lady who had been praying it over her 12-year-old son, who she believed had been misdiagnosed with Attention Deficit Disorder (ADD). The doctors and her husband had been pressing for the child to be medicated, much to the consternation of both mother and son, who were adamant that God was going to help him. But medical science prevailed, and two attempts had been initiated to change the child's behavior with drugs to no avail. Finally, the parents were led to have the boy's vision tested and found out that all he really needs is vision therapy to correct a problem with the way his brain is processing visual information. The mom believes this is a direct result of the backdoor prayer!

Practical Application:

Consider ways in which the events of your daily life may interact with and/or be impacted by your dreams. Ponder the question, "If this was a dream, what would it mean?"

[1] Job 33:14-17a

[2] Romans 8:5-8

[3] Philippians 4:8

[4] Dawn Bray is a prayer minister and prophetic intercessor, a good friend of Aslan's Place

CHAPTER EIGHTEEN
EVANGELISM

That the Bible is the final authority in regard to everything we understand about God cannot be overstated or repeated too many times. Once again, we go there; this time to validate the importance of dreams in terms of evangelism.

History remembers King Nebuchadnezzar as the greatest king of ancient Babylon, a blatantly pagan king who prayed to the gods. He defeated the Egyptians and Assyrians, subdued Palestine and Syria, controlled all trade routes across Mesopotamia, and is credited with cultural and intellectual pursuits that eclipse any others of his day.[1] But then along came Daniel, a young Jewish captive to whom God had given understanding of dreams and visions.[2] Can there be any doubt that his interpretations of the king's disturbing dreams contributed to Nebuchadnezzar's radical change from a man who required his subjects to worship him[3] to a humbled king who professed the greatness of our God?

> *King Nebuchadnezzar to all peoples, nations, and languages, that dwell in all the earth: Peace be multiplied to you. It has seemed good to me to show the signs and wonders that the Most High God has done for me. How great are his signs, how mighty his wonders! His kingdom is an everlasting kingdom, and his dominion endures from generation to generation.*
>
> *I, Nebuchadnezzar, was at ease in my house and prospering in my palace. I saw a dream that made me afraid. As I lay in bed the fancies and the visions of my head alarmed me…At last Daniel came in before me…*
>
> *…this is the interpretation, O king: It is a decree of the Most High, which has come upon my lord the king, that you shall be driven from among men, and your dwelling shall be with the beasts of the field. You shall be made to eat grass like an ox, and you shall be wet with the dew of heaven, and seven periods of time shall pass over you, till you know that the Most High rules the kingdom of men*

and gives it to whom he will…All this came upon King Nebuchadnezzar.

At the end of the days I, Nebuchadnezzar, lifted my eyes to heaven, and my reason returned to me, and I blessed the Most High, and praised and honored him who lives forever, for his dominion is an everlasting dominion, and his kingdom endures from generation to generation; all the inhabitants of the earth are accounted as nothing, and he does according to his will among the host of heaven and among the inhabitants of the earth; and none can stay his hand or say to him, "What have you done?"

At the same time my reason returned to me, and for the glory of my kingdom, my majesty and splendor returned to me. My counselors and my lords sought me, and I was established in my kingdom, and still more greatness was added to me. Now I, Nebuchadnezzar, praise and extol and honor the King of heaven, for all his works are right and his ways are just; and those who walk in pride he is able to humble.[4]

Fast forward well over a half century to Paul's call to evangelism in a land that required a land-and-sea journey of 150 miles:[5]

And a vision appeared to Paul in the night: a man of Macedonia was standing there, urging him and saying, "Come over to Macedonia and help us." And when Paul had seen the vision, immediately we sought to go on into Macedonia, concluding that God had called us to preach the gospel to them.[6]

OK, but that was then and this is now so what do dreams have in common with evangelism today? A lot! It's crystal clear that our God never changes and that He still speaks to us through dreams and visions, so it should also be clear that unbelievers might still be convicted and Christians may still be directed to share the gospel through Dreamspeak.

Perhaps you're familiar with the multitude of accounts coming out of Muslim areas of how God has used people's dreams to draw them to Himself. I'm always blessed to read such testimonies, and I pray the one that follows will bless you.

My friend, Ehsan, was born in Cairo, Egypt soon after it had transitioned, first from a monarchy to a republic, and then to a dictatorship. She grew up under a system of political persecution, amidst a growing hatred for Israel. It was not until the Six Day War between Israel and its neighbors, Egypt, Jordan and Syria that her mother revealed her Jewish identity and the fact that her sister had lived in Israel with her family since 1948. Married to Ehsan's father, a Muslim man, she had felt the need to protect her child and had hidden her true identity for many years. Ehsan continues:

> As a child, I had a dream at a time when both my family and the country were facing troubled times. In my dream I was in a jungle being chased by what appeared to be savage, indigenous people, but suddenly I found myself in a desert facing a shepherd with white hair. I looked into his deep brown eyes and asked, "How come you saved me since I am not a Christian?" He answered, "I save everybody." Even as a child, I knew that he was a Christian.
>
> A few years later I went with a Catholic friend to her church and remember experiencing a peace that I'd never felt before. Drawn to both the cross and the silence, I also felt that there was something special about Jesus that I couldn't understand.
>
> In 1980, six years after I immigrated to Canada, I had an encounter with Jesus. Seated in half lotus position and meditating on universal love, the thought of Jesus suddenly came to my mind and I felt a supernatural love that was so intense that I was drawn to his person.
>
> A few weeks passed before I met a friend that I hadn't seen for a year. She witnessed about her born again Christian experience, and I received Jesus as my personal Savior.

Ehsan has matured into a woman of astounding faith. What a journey! From a little girl subjected to the rigid control of Islam, totally unaware of either her Jewish heritage or the Man who would become her Savior, to the woman who is an incredible blessing to many.

Practical Application:

Pray for unbelievers to experience dreams and visions that will lead them into a relationship with God. When a non-Christian appears in your dreams, consider how God might be leading you to pray for or minister to them.

[1] http://www.ancient.eu/Nebuchadnezzar_II/

[2] Daniel 1:17

[3] Daniel 3

[4] Daniel 4:1-5, 8a, 24-25, 28, 34-37

[5]http://www.biblecharts.org/newtestaament/paulssecondmissionaryjourney.pdf

[6] Acts 16:9-10

CHAPTER NINETEEN
BEHOLD, HE COMES

Perhaps you're familiar with Donnie McClurkin's wonderful song, *Days of Elijah*. Taken directly from Revelation 1:7, the first line of the refrain is, "Behold He comes, riding on the clouds…" It's enough to "shiver me timbers," as Long John Silver or Popeye would have exclaimed to express fear or awe.[1] Yes, Jesus will return one day, riding on the clouds; but in the meantime He often comes in our dreams, and when He does there are no words to adequately describe how truly awesome it is.

I have personally encountered Jesus in dreams on numerous occasions, undoubtedly much more often than is recalled due the quickly fading nature of dreams. But, like the two on the road to Emmaus,[2] I usually didn't recognize Him until 'my eyes were opened'. On one occasion though, Jesus' identity was certain, and we were both laughing as He performed the greatest-ever teppanyaki chef act, tossing knives in the air with abandon. I remember exclaiming, "It's a good thing you're God, or you could really hurt yourself!" He just laughed and then showed me how to cut just a few slices of a piece of calamari. I expected it to be tough because of a recent experience while preparing a rubbery calamari steak for dinner, but it was so easy that I got carried away and quickly sliced up the whole thing, only to look up and see Him walking away. Devastated, I cried, "Come back!" But He just kept on walking, and I woke up with the sad knowledge, and a lifelong lesson learned, that it's never a good idea to get ahead of God, but to do only that which He asks. I hope to never again watch as He walks away from me!

On May 30, 2003, I had been actively pursuing intimacy with God for several years but was still a 'babe in the woods' in terms of the things of the Spirit, especially in terms of the unseen reality of the spiritual realms. As yet, I had no clue that they are actually the larger reality than the physical realm in which we live. While journaling my prayers each day, I wrote down a dream, not because

I knew I should but because it seemed so important to talk to the Lord about it:

> I've never had any dream messages or visions from You, at least none that I've recognized, and I'm not going to worry or dwell on this. If You have something there for me to see, I'm willing for You to show me, and I'll listen for your voice. But, if it's just me imagining, trying to read something into it that's not there, it'll just remain in these pages and fade away.

But it was never forgotten, and it came back to me time and again until I finally understood. The journal continued:

> I was in a room with other people—I don't remember how many. There were some small windows along one wall, and at the end of the room a big picture window with a window shade that was pulled all the way up. Quite unexpectedly, it started to snow outside and everyone was pretty excited. The others were looking out the smaller windows, but I was the only one who thought to look out of the big window. Then it started snowing really hard, and for some reason the others left the room, except for one man somewhere in the background, but I can't remember who it was or exactly when I knew the person was there. The snow was coming down so hard that it covered everything around in just a few minutes, deepening by several inches every few seconds, piling up so fast on the outside of the window that it would soon have covered the building. I suddenly knew without a doubt that it was evil and rebuked Satan in Jesus' name, and immediately the snow stopped. My first reaction was fear of Satan's power, but that was quickly followed by awe at my ability to make him stop. I wasn't comfortable with what had happened because it was so big and scary, but right away I knew that I didn't have to be afraid because of You. I left the room and went into another part of the building that was large and open with lots of windows, and it was bright and sunny and green outside.

> There was no snow except a little around the foundation of that one room, but it quickly tapered off to green grass and I knew that the rest of it would soon melt away and be gone.

An interesting note was recorded about three weeks later on June 22, "…in the dream it happened so fast, and it was after-the-fact that I felt scared—but You immediately reassured me that there was no need to be afraid because I have you." Pondering the dream, I recalled many dreams over the years in which I would rebuke Satan, but didn't remember any like this where the effect was immediate. I told the Lord, "Only you know what you've been doing to prepare me." But prepare me for what? I still didn't know.

Eventually, I came to understand that this was a 'calling dream'. This time, it wasn't Jesus who was there, but was His Spirit—the Holy Spirit—who often enters our dreams as someone unrecognized and is likely to be standing behind us. Little did I know that I would eventually come to Aslan's Place, become a prayer minister, routinely act in Jesus' name and observe the enemy flee, and understand the authority I have in Christ Jesus, let alone write books about it!

In the *Conversations* chapter, I shared how Jesus once came; looking like David might have appeared. In 2006, he showed up in a scary dream dressed as a maintenance man! But we'll get to that one in the next chapter.

As always, what's the biblical evidence that God, whether as Father, Son or Holy Spirit, will appear in dreams and visions? Abimelech's you're-a-dead-man dream is one example, but we can also look at a warning God delivered to Jacob's father-in-law:

> *But God came to Laban the Aramean in a dream by night and said to him, "Be careful not to say anything to Jacob, either good or bad."* [3]

Finally, who could forget the astounding visions of the Lord that were experienced by Stephen and the apostles, Paul and John?

And he said, "Behold, I see the heavens opened, and the Son of Man standing at the right hand of God." [4]

Now as he went on his way, he approached Damascus, and suddenly a light from heaven shone around him. And falling to the ground, he heard a voice saying to him, "Saul, Saul, why are you persecuting me?" And he said, "Who are you, Lord?" And he said, "I am Jesus, whom you are persecuting. But rise and enter the city, and you will be told what you are to do." The men who were traveling with him stood speechless, hearing the voice but seeing no one.[5]

At once I was in the Spirit, and behold, a throne stood in heaven, with one seated on the throne. And he who sat there had the appearance of jasper and carnelian, and around the throne was a rainbow that had the appearance of an emerald…And between the throne and the four living creatures and among the elders I saw a Lamb standing, as though it had been slain, with seven horns and with seven eyes, which are the seven spirits of God sent out into all the earth.[6]

It's clear that God does visit us in dreams and visions. We would do well to be alert for them so we don't miss a divine encounter.

Practical Application:

Consider instances when the Jesus may have shown up in your dreams as well as times when there was an unidentified individual, the Holy Spirit, in the background. What were they doing? Consider the significance of seeing the Lord in a dream. How does it change your outlook on life?

1 https://en.wikipedia.org/wiki/Shiver_my_timbers

2 Luke 24:13-35

3 Genesis 31:24

4 Acts 6:56

5 Acts 9:3-7

6 Revelation 4:2-3; Revelation 5:6

CHAPTER TWENTY
GUIDANCE AND ENCOURAGEMENT

Snakes…I HATE SNAKES!!! Needless to say, I wasn't enjoying my dream of three ugly black ones threatening me. Little did I know when I awoke that morning, trembling with fear, that by nightfall I would be praising God for it.

It was an epic kind of dream with at least eight different scenes, and it occurred the night before an appointment with my oncologist to discuss treatment options for breast cancer. The first surgical pathology report had come back less encouraging than expected, so he gave me all the statistics regarding re-occurrence and long-term survival. For the type and size of cancer, the percentage of difference between having chemotherapy or not were very small, so it was a difficult decision. The doctor wasn't much help; he wouldn't tell me what to do; it had to be my decision. Home I went, armed with statistics, to talk it over with my family, but they didn't have any clear answers either. At some point I remembered the dream, and when I went back and looked at what I'd written down that very morning I was astounded. The overall context of the dream implied that I was on some type of journey and, while I really couldn't see where I was going, as long as I kept my eyes fixed on the Lord I would arrive safely at my destination. There was even a knowing in the dream that I needed to be somewhere at 3:45 PM—I didn't know where but I knew it was important. Only in retrospect did I realize that my doctor's appointment had been at 3:45 PM that day. So, back to the snakes:

> Alone in a bed in the living room, I saw three snakes that had been contained in a glass aquarium in the corner, but two had escaped. A man came in but quickly left, saying he'd send someone else back to take care of it. The second man, dressed like a maintenance man, came in armed only with a belt in his hand. I was pretty worried; how in the world was he going to protect me with a belt??? In the meantime, snake number one had

> disappeared into the room somewhere. I wondered again how the man could possibly do anything with a belt, but he cornered snake number two and made it get back into the aquarium. It escaped again though, and I was really upset because it was very long and dangerous-looking. Surprisingly, the man didn't seem at all concerned as He continued to do battle with snake number three; it was the worst; big, and black, and very ugly. Then it reared up over the top of the aquarium and puffed up like a cobra with its wide, hooded head and hate-filled eyes, spitting and striking at everything in reach. The top was still not on the aquarium and I was terrified that it was going to escape and come after me. Its head kept coming way up over the rim before the man would beat it back down again with his belt, yet he glanced casually over his shoulder at me and said with a shrug, as if it were no big deal, "Death is really mad today."

When I started seeking the Lord regarding the meaning of the dream it became clear that the first snake was the tumor that had already been removed so it had disappeared. The second snake was the threat of metastasis, and the third was death. It became clear that God was showing me to go ahead with the chemotherapy and I felt his assurance that if I did, snake number two didn't have a chance. But then it got really good because the Holy Spirit showed me that Jesus himself (and, even now, I get tears in my eyes just writing about it) was the man who came to me in the dream with His belt of truth in hand to restrain death. Wow! I'd read many times about the armor of God, but now had seen its power in action!

> *...finally, be strong in the Lord and in his mighty power. Put on the full armor of God so that you can take your stand against the devil's schemes. For our struggle is not against flesh and blood, but against the rulers, against the authorities, against the powers of this dark world and against the spiritual forces of evil in the heavenly realms. Therefore put on the full armor of God, so that when the day of evil comes, you may be able to stand your ground, and after you have done everything, to stand. Stand firm then, with the belt of truth buckled*

> *around your waist, with the breastplate of righteousness in place, and with your feet fitted with the readiness that comes from the gospel of peace. In addition to all this, take up the shield of faith, with which you can extinguish all the flaming arrows of the evil one. Take the helmet of salvation and the sword of the Spirit, which is the word of God.*

Just imagine the protection that is available to us if we're wearing the full set of armor when Truth is all it takes to restrain Death!

Though many often insist that God no longer speaks in dreams, there's no way anyone will ever convince me of that. Over and over he has comforted me and provided direction during the night hours, as some other journal entries during the year of cancer treatment indicate:

> In a dream this morning, I was identified as one of God's elect, with the ability to encounter the realm of the Spirit and to find rest there. Praying about it, I was led to an encouraging word from the Apostle Peter that was written to people who were living as foreigners in distant lands:
>
> > *God the Father knew you and chose you long ago, and his Spirit has made you holy. As a result, you have obeyed him and have been cleansed by the blood of Jesus Christ. May God give you more and more grace and peace.* [1]
>
> How interesting that my name, Barbara, literally means foreigner or stranger; and yes, I am a stranger here; in this world but not of this world, and much loved by my Father.
>
> I don't understand all that transpired last night, but when I fell asleep in a chair in my living room I went somewhere else, into another dimension, and I literally felt myself taking off. While there, a man who seemed like a dear old friend came to me; he was so familiar, and we were both so happy to see each other again. I asked if we were together in body or in spirit and he just smiled and

> said, "What do you think?" I don't know what else may have occurred between us, but at one point he said, "Cut that off," and used his hand to cut off something I couldn't see. I've often wondered who this was—could it have been my great-grandfather, the circuit riding preacher from the early 1900s whom I never met? I don't know, but he knew me and loved me, and I had the sense that he was removing a generational issue. Just as I was beginning to wake up, I peeked to see where I was and saw a vision of a couple of old, black-and-white televisions with pictures flickering on the screens. I said, "Lord, if this is not supposed to be, let it stop" and both immediately quit; the one closest to me just seemed to fizzle out. Also, a large collection of junk lying was lying around but suddenly it all disappeared and the entire floor was covered in new potting soil. God has done a work in me during the night and I'm on new ground; the way is cleared for a new thing to grow. Yes! Thank-you Lord!

On my dad's eighty-first birthday (how I love God's timing!), I received an amazing gift. Another dream—an assurance that the victory had been won and that the cancer curse was dead. It was another epic, and I seemed to be battling an evil martial artist all night long. He was so powerful that none could stand before his skill or his weaponry, but I kept evading him somehow. Finally, his evil became so intense that he was destroying even his own warriors, and just when it appeared that there was no more hope for me, one of his own weapons turned upon him and he was suddenly nothing more than a pile of sawdust. The scene changed and a deliveryman came to the door and handed me three take-out-food containers. The first container was empty; the second was empty; the third held the sawdust. I woke up and instantly knew that all three snakes had been defeated—the tumor was gone; any metastatic disease was gone; and death had been defeated—nothing but dust with no power to harm me. I remembered that Jesus is Truth, and Death cannot stand against him. A few days later, the Lord gave me the perfect verse to sum it all up:

There they are in great terror, for God is with the generation of the righteous.[2]

It just doesn't get any better than that.

Practical Application:

Think about dreams in which you received guidance or encouragement. Journal the difference those dreams made in your life and spend some time thanking and praising God for His intervention.

[1] 1 Peter 1:1-2

[2] Psalm 14:5

CHAPTER TWENTY-ONE
'DEAD DREAMS'

In general, dreams and visions about death are rarely about actual physical death. Most often, they are about death to something of the world, or the end of something old so a new thing can be birthed (i.e., a job or other activity, a standard practice, etc.).

Occasionally though, a dream about death is just that. Perhaps you recall that Abraham Lincoln shared with friends a dream in which he'd walked into the East Room of the White House to find a covered corpse, guarded by soldiers and surrounded by mourners. When he asked who had died, a soldier replied, "The president. He was killed by an assassin."[1] We all know how that turned out!

During a webinar, participants were invited to send in dreams to analyze and share. A lady asked for help with one that a friend had experienced, the friend being an elderly lady who kept insisting that she knew through a dream that she would die soon. She was quite happy about it and ready to go, having lived a full and satisfying life. However, our participant was desperately hoping to receive an encouraging interpretation so she could go back and talk the lady out of her sense of impending death. Having just taught that such dreams are usually not literal, my first thought was that this would illustrate that. Then I prayerfully read through the dream, and try as I might, nothing came to me except that this was a exactly what it appeared to be, and was probably meant to allow the elderly woman to encourage and say goodbye to her loved ones, put her affairs in order, and then leave with grace at God's appointed time. I never heard what happened and I certainly could have been wrong, but my guess is that the lady soon went home, full of joy and knowing that she would soon look into the face of Jesus, which was her earnest desire.

Biblically, we know that such foreknowledge of the threat of death can be from God, and not just fear mongering by the enemy. Moses was clearly told exactly when and where he would die,[2] and Abimelech's 'behold, you're a dead-man dream' would certainly have been fulfilled had he violated Sarah.[3]

I had two dreams that were definitely about death regarding my husband, but didn't connect the dots between them for years. The first was in 2004, just prior to an emergency pacemaker, without which he would have died within a very short time. The second was in 2008, when my husband was in Pennsylvania on business and I was in North Carolina for an Aslan's Place School of Ministry, very far removed from one another and from our California home and doctors. One morning I awoke feeling very unsettled because I'd seen him lying in a coffin. I checked with a friend who was a dream interpreter, but she was busy and brushed it off with a usual by-the-book assumption. I figured she knew more than me, so I put it in the back of my mind and went to the morning session.

Several hours later, Paul taught about entering into God's rest and all of us laid down on the floor, soaking to the *The Song of Angels* by Freddie Hayler. The music ended and Paul dismissed everyone for lunch, but I felt that I needed to remain on the floor as worship tunes continued to play. That lasted about 30 minutes, with my only sense of anything being the need to wait on the Lord. Finally, I felt released to get up and go into the other room to get some lunch. My hunger satisfied, I remembered that my phone was muted and it would be a good idea to check for messages. To my shock, there was one from a PA emergency room saying to call immediately because my husband was headed into surgery. Fortunately, the following message was an ER doctor telling me that my husband was now OK. 'Immediately' is not sufficient to describe the speed with which I returned that call, learning that Jack had become dizzy at work and had fallen and hit his head. The first aid responder had been concerned and called 911, and the paramedics rushed him to the hospital with his heart barely beating. Once there, he'd arrested and had to be resuscitated. A pacemaker wire had gone bad and had been replaced, and he was now stable. It didn't take long to recognize the timeline. The first call had come as I lay on the floor alone, and I didn't see the message until there was an all clear. Immediately knew two things: first, God had demonstrated His miraculous life-saving power to care for my husband while I waited in His rest, completely unconcerned;

second, the dream hadn't been a run-of-the-mill textbook 'dead dream' at all. Sometime later, I was astounded to discover that the first dream from years before happened just prior to our first experience of getting to the hospital in the nick of time!

Conversation with others has revealed that many people have dreamed they saw themselves as dead bodies and then realized their dreams were a confirmation of a major decision to consciously and willingly die to the things of the world. My journal reveals my dream from July 2003:

> I was alive, yet my body was dead, my corpse lying on a gurney in a hospital, covered with a sheet. Very interested in seeing what it looked like, I asked to take a look at myself. Appearing very peaceful, I was quite dead, with a huge, gaping, bloody hole in the upper abdomen. I felt absolutely fine about it, knowing that it was the old me, dead to the world but alive to Christ.

> *Set your minds on things that are above, not on things that are on earth. For you have died, and your life is hidden with Christ in God.*[4]

The dream encouraged me to always remember my commitment to die to the world, and was so necessary over the next few years as I had to let go of, or die to, more things over and over again.

Practical Application:

Be careful not to assume a textbook interpretation is correct, regardless of the type of dream. Always, always, ask the Lord first and prayerfully consider the message in every dream.

[1] http://www.history.com/news/ask-history/did-abraham-lincoln-predict-his-own-death

[2] Deuteronomy 34

[3] Genesis 20

[4] Colossians 3:2-3

CHAPTER TWENTY-TWO
A LAND BEFORE TIME

In 1985, the enduring tale of Marty McFly (Michael J Fox) and Doc (Christopher Lloyd) zooming backward and forward in time hit the theaters, and *Back to the Future* seemingly became an instance classic. But why not? Such a possibility has long captivated man. The enduring tale of H. G. Wells, *The Time Machine*, was written in 1895—long before any of us were born. Yet it has re-surfaced over and over ever since in one adaptation after another, most recently (as of this writing) in NBC's television show, *Timeless.*

Why are we so interested in time travel? Is it possible that there exists within us not only a desire to explore, but to go back and experience that which we have known before?

At the moment of conception we entered into the physical reality of time and space, but it is clear that our spirits pre-existed our conception and birth, for how can one remember that which has not been previously known, or return to a place one has never been?

> *Remember also your Creator in the days of your youth, before…the dust returns to the earth as it was, and the spirit returns to God who gave it.*[1]

Additionally, we were predestined in love for the fulfillment of God's purposes before the foundation of the world[2] and God knew us well, even before the formation of our physical bodies.[3]

Remember how Elisha persistently followed Elijah in spite of his instruction to stay behind? Over and over, Elijah said, "Please stay here," but Elisha passionately wanted the blessing he knew he could receive so he doggedly followed everywhere his master went.[4] I had a similar experience on July 4, 2014:

> Last night was difficult but I'm sure, important. Sleep was frequently interrupted; the Spirit was moving as I was

> pressing into something I do not know. During the first hours of the night, I was seeing and hearing snippets of things and kept coming into agreement with whatever God was doing. There were several hours in which it felt as if I was flying high, but also going deep; all was dark; perseverance was required. It would've been so easy to give up and get up, but I knew I had to press in. Finally, around 4:30 or 5 AM, I saw a skyline with a beautiful sunrise beginning, and from above I looked down to see huge swelling waves, probably twenty to thirty feet high. The giant waves were not because of a storm, and they illustrated majestic power of God magnificently. Then I woke up, knowing I'd made some kind of breakthrough but wondering what that was.

Months later, on February 25, 2015, I wrote an email to Paul:

> Oh my, I am in absolute shock! I was thinking about my vision of what I finally realized much later was the womb of the dawn, and went looking for it. I am astounded that it happened last 4th of July, not only Independence Day, but also the day before my birthday!!!

Eventually I understood that in my journey to the womb of the dawn[5] I was re-visiting an old and familiar place. Our pre-existence explains why it's not uncommon in a dream to recognize a setting, an experience, or a person we've never encountered while awake.

The question becomes, how much of what is revealed through dreams and visions is actually a prompt to remember something our spirits have always known rather than new information? Are we truly traveling back to 'a land before time'? It's definitely something to think about because whether our journey is a prophetic trip to the future or a retrospective trip to the past, our ability to experience both is not the science fiction of *Back to the Future* or *The Time Machine*. How can that be? It's actually very simple—our God is not confined to time, so in Him, neither are we! The big difference though, is that we do not designate or initiate our time travel. He does, and we just get to go along for the ride!

Since God is not limited by time or space, in Him we are free to follow His Spirit into the heavenly places and explore dimensions that will teach us more about astounding aspects of our God and His creation such as we've never…hmmm, I almost wrote, "never dreamed." That would've been wrong because that which we've never known may well be encountered in our dreams.

Practical Application:

Try to recognize Dreamspeak clues indicating that you've gone somewhere outside of the time indicated on your alarm clock. Have you gone backward or forward, or are you outside of time looking in from another dimension? Do you recognize a setting, experience, or individual that you know you've never encountered before in the physical realm?

[1] Ecclesiastes 12:1a, 7

[2] Ephesians 1:4-5

[3] Psalm 139:15-16

[4] 1 Kings 2

[5] Psalm 110:3

CHAPTER TWENTY-THREE
REFLECTIONS

Can you imagine how the smooth surface of a pristine lake can reflect the image of a magnificent snow-capped mountain and its surrounding scenery? All of us have seen such pictures, but they fall far short of actually being there. Without the physical discernment of climate, or sights, sounds and smells, the overall experience cannot truly be enjoyed except in the imagination. Likewise, a crisp, clear photograph that reflects the absolute cuteness of my grandchildren will undoubtedly tug at both my heartstrings and the corners of my mouth as I break into a delighted smile, but it doesn't allow me to hear their laughter and scoop them into my arms in delight. These are just reflections of a much bigger three-dimensional reality.

Dreams reflect the bigger spiritual reality that encompasses multitudes of dimensions lying far beyond our comprehension. There is a lot more that could be written about my own thoughts and experiences; so much in fact, that this book could be extended far beyond the length the Lord is indicating. As a result, this chapter will offer a few brief, but hopefully thought-provoking observations for the reader to ponder and pursue independently. After all, the intent of this book is to encourage individual pursuit of each person's own Dreamspeak experience, recalling Paul's definition from Chapter 1 that it is a language known only by you and God.

Gates

As Jacob was fleeing from Esau, he was stepping off into an unknown wilderness on his journey to Haran. Then God gave him the dream, popularly known as 'Jacob's Ladder', in which he saw angels ascending and descending from heaven and the Lord standing at the top, declaring the Abrahamic covenantal promise to him personally for the first time.[1] His experience indicates that our dreams are gates through which we can enter into a spiritual reality:

> *And he was afraid and said, "How awesome is this place! This is none other than the house of God, and this is the gate of heaven."* [2]

We must examine our dreams carefully and learn to go beyond them, stepping into the higher reality that is set before us.

Layers

Like scriptures, dreams often appear to have many layers, and with the benefit of hindsight we may encounter meanings that have developed over time, or new insights we've never noticed before. I've often heard dreams compared to the layers of an onion; you peel one off and is there more underneath. Personally, I'd rather think of them as ice cream cakes with layer after layer of delicious tidbits from the Lord to savor and digest.

Why Prophetic Dreams?

Scripture is clear that God often shows previews of coming events to His people:

> *For the Lord God does nothing without revealing his secret to his servants the prophets.* [3]

But why would he reveal the future? There are some easy answers, the most obvious of which is so we can be prepared and can pray into situations on the horizon. But, how about this as a thought to ponder? Could it be that in our dreams and visions we actually see what is already happening in spiritual realms and advancing toward the physical so we will be able to understand when it happens? How does this play into the concept of us co-operating with God to usher in His will on earth as it already is in heaven, as we are instructed in the Lord's Prayer?[4]

Remembering the Future

Having spoken of both retrospective and prophetic time travel through the vehicle of dreams and visions, there remains another question to ponder. Is it possible that we can remember the future as we do the past?

There is no doubt that the Apostle John's prophetic vision of Revelation is astounding. It offers instruction for the Church regarding conforming to God's standard's of righteousness as well as extraordinary visual images of what is yet to come. Was he simply seeing into the future, or had he been taken there and was now remembering it?

I once had a very realistic vision that was set within the context of a longer dream. I saw some of the events of Revelation playing out before me in the very same way John must have experienced them, and it literally felt as if I were there. However, unlike John, once awake I knew that my experience had been very real but couldn't recall the details except to know that it had been exactly as he described. After the vision the dream had continued, and I watched from a hiding place, terrified that I would be seen because the black horse and his rider were walking down the street. The horse was so tall that I could only see up to the stirrups, about the level of a three-story building. I knew without a doubt that the black horse roaming the earth was present tense; but the Revelation vision had been very different, as if I was there. Did I remember the future? Or, did I simply see into the future as well as the present? Could I have been transported into the future, and then returned to observe the present? I don't know for sure, but in God the possibilities are undoubtedly endless.

Those Who Have Gone Before

In our dreams we often encounter friends and family members who have already left this realm and entered into eternity with God. Sometimes it's clear that they are symbolic of another person, time or event, and when correctly interpreted their presence grants insight into the intended message of Dreamspeak. But can we actually interact with those who have now joined the Cloud of Witnesses? I think we can and we do, probably more often than we realize, for they are now more alive than they ever were in the physical and there is biblical precedent that there can be encounters with them, including Saul's experience with the Witch of Endor calling up Samuel after he died,[5] and Jesus on the Mount of Transfiguration with Moses and Elijah.[6]

I was attending an Aslan's Place summit in March 2017, and there were friends from all over—Rob Gross was there from Hawaii, and there were also people from New England, Minnesota, Texas and many other places. On the first day as we greeted one another, the usual question was, "How are you?" I had a choice; say I'm fine, or just answer, "OK," because I really didn't feel fine but didn't know why. I decided to be honest and their response was consistent, "Why just OK? What's wrong?" I had no answer. On the second day, while speaking to an old friend, I suddenly began to understand what was happening and entered into a whole new level with God. From my journal:

> It turns out that my flat-line affect of yesterday was grief! Today is the eighth anniversary of Dad's passing, and I recalled my dream from a week ago in which I saw him and said, "You know you're here on assignment." He just grinned and said, "Yes." I didn't know what that was all about but once I realized what day this is, I started processing its significance. Meanwhile, Rob was speaking and as soon as he mentioned, "Father's heart" I burst out of a realm of grief I didn't even know I carried and into the realm of majesty, which included tremendous joy bubbling up like a fountain. The whole group entered into a time of worship, which was especially wonderful for me now. Afterward, sitting back down to listen to the next speaker, I just knew I had to figure out how to get Dad's picture off the Amazon cloud and post it on Facebook to honor his memory and remind my family of my amazing father. At the same time, I could feel his presence, complete with that sweet grin, right there in the room with me. It was like nothing I have ever experienced before!
>
> God, my God, You are amazing; and I'm sorry I was so upset that I was so down the last couple of days. I should have known that You were up to something! Wow, wow, wow!!!!

Perhaps the grief was also because this day was the eleventh anniversary of my surgery for breast cancer, a date that marks the beginning of one of the most difficult year's of my life. It really doesn't matter though, because whether it was the cancer or the loss of my dad I didn't even know I'd been carrying grief. But God did, and how like Him to send my Dad to help usher in this new celebration of joy!

Intersections of Time and Space

When numbers appear in a dream they may be literal or symbolic. Often, the interpretation revolves around a commonly understood meaning of a number (i.e., 5 = grace), or it can be found in a scripture reference by looking up the various chapter-and-verse combinations that are possible (i.e., 23 = 23rd Psalm, or 316 = John 3:16). That said, God tends to get very creative with Dreamspeak and there's no limit to what he might come up with—perhaps speed limits, or ages, or dollars and cents—the possibilities are endless.

Recently, a friend had a dream in which he felt a number represented a moment on the clock that was a gate into time, so I started thinking of what potential ramifications of that might be. It occurred to me that at every minute that is divisible by 5, there is an instant when the hour, minute and second hands all come together as one, or in unity. If each of those intersections of time represent a time gate, then what would they mean if this were a dream?

If numbers are interpreted in terms of a clock face rather than a scripture or something else, they could take on the meaning of the numbers plus time, and perhaps indicate a gate into the dimension of time. So, applying common numerical meanings to the twelve intersections,[7] each one could illustrate a wonderfully prophetic message. Just two examples: 1:05 could mean a full complement (100) of God's grace (5); 8:40 might indicate a new beginning (8) coming into alignment with the completion of a time of testing (40).

Since nothing is always and we can't put God's creativity in a box, so ask the Lord, and expand your thinking out of a pre-determined definition in the number section of a dream dictionary.

In Jesus' Words

In the following verses, Jesus didn't mention dreams specifically, but his words certainly apply to them:

> *For the Father loves the Son and shows him all that he himself is doing. And greater works than these will he show him, so that you may marvel.*[8]

> *Truly, truly, I say to you, whoever believes in me will also do the works that I do; and greater works than these will he do, because I am going to the Father.*[9]

We have to observe something first, before we put it into practice. Dreams allow us to see things so we can then walk them out in daily life. Understanding Dreamspeak will play a large part in the greater works that I believe we can expect to see one day soon.

Practical Application:

Begin a list of your own reflections about Dreamspeak. Include insights as well as questions you'd like to have answered. Then, talk to the Lord about it; research your questions just as you would a particular dream; and ask trusted friends for assistance.

[1] Genesis 28

[2] Genesis 28:17 NLT

[3] Amos 3:7

[4] Matthew 6:9-13

[5] 1 Samuel 28

[6] Matthew 17 & Luke 9

[7] 1:05, 2:10, 3:15, 4:20, 5:25, 6:30, 7:35, 8:40, 9:45, 10:50, 11:55, 12:00

[8] John 5:20

[9] John 14:12

CHAPTER TWENTY-FOUR
TESTIMONIES

Who doesn't love a good story, especially when it is an encouraging one? The early church was privileged to hear some great first-hand accounts about Jesus from those who had known him as he walked the earth:

> *And with great power the apostles were giving their testimony to the resurrection of the Lord Jesus, and great grace was upon them all.*[1]

The good news for us is that though Jesus is no longer here physically, His Spirit continues His work in and through us; and current testimonies of the astounding works of God are still thrilling to hear, or read in this case.

I asked a few people who have experienced wonderful blessings from the Lord through the understanding of their dreams to share their stories. I pray you will enjoy them as much as I do.

Sanji relates her testimony about how God encouraged her through Dreamspeak:

> In a very difficult period of my life I was fasting and praying for the Lord to show me what is going on in my life. I started having dreams during the night and early waking hours of the morning. Some were repeated and I wanted to know what they meant—I needed an interpretation. I tried different methods and spent a lot of time, but could not get a clear answer. I was very familiar with stories from my Sunday school days in years gone by where I learned about the dreams of such people as Jacob, Joseph, Pharaoh, Daniel, Nebuchadnezzar, Solomon, and the Joseph of the New Testament. I knew that as God was telling them something, He was also speaking to me.
>
> So I went on a three-day time of fasting and prayer and asked the Lord to either tell me what He was saying or

> lead me to a believer who was led by the Word of God and the Holy Spirit. I was desperate to know what was in God's mind. On the third day in the mid-afternoon I was led to Barbara, who helped me interpret my dreams by asking Jesus and following the leading of the Holy Spirit. We still correspond regularly.
>
> The dream interpretations have warned me and guided me through the most critical situations of my life. They have helped me to make the right decisions and choices and have changed my perspective of life. Without the Lord's leading through my dreams I would have chosen the world's way instead of God's way.
>
> I have learned to always ask Jesus to come into in a dream that I've had and show me where He was and what He was doing in it, as well as what he thought about the situation and what he wanted me to know. This helped me tremendously to learn to trust Him as my main source for interpreting my dreams, with the Holy Spirit leading the way to open the eyes of my mind to His truth.
>
> The dream interpretations have changed the outlook of my Christian life as I have learned to live as though Jesus is right there with me all the time, to invite Him into every situation of my life, and ask Him what He would like do, or what he would like me to do in my situation. I've learned to follow His leading and He continually teaches me to trust Him and His Word more and more.
>
> Several dreams were promises that have encouraged me to live with boldness and without fear because the Lord was with me through the entire process. I am certain that He will lead me to fulfill His divine plan and purpose for my life.

Bella is a fifteen-year-old high school student who is living proof that God is not a respecter of age in terms of whom He speaks to in dreams. We were together in my car with her mom, driving to a seminar when she shared a dream that she didn't understand:

> We went to school in a strip mall. There was a kid in my class who gave me a ring. The ring was a rough, cement-like material that was all jagged. It had a blue stone that was a rectangle with a triangle at each end (like a side of a crystal). I put the ring on and immediately fell to the floor. I could not see.

Driving along, I led Bella through a quick generational deliverance prayer to cancel any evil that was coming against her vision. Later, her mom reported:

> Prior to this dream, Bella had a few dreams where she could not see clearly. Things were blurry or fuzzy, but after the prayer ministry she now has many dreams and they are never blurry. It's as if she can now see clearly in the spiritual realm.

Rhonda shares her experience regarding a dream with an interpretation that didn't make too much sense initially, but became evident over time. This was a prophetic warning or 'heads-up' dream that prepared her to understand what she would soon begin to observe.

> I had a dream that concerned me because it had to do with a friend of mine so I asked Barbara about it. In the dream my friend was very sick (we went to the same church at the time in the natural), and the church kept praying for her but she would not get better. This woman is a very godly woman and I could not understand why she would not get better when they prayed for her.
>
> Barbara shared that a woman often represents the church and that the dream indicated a sick church. At the time, I thought, "That's interesting. I like the church, but it does have a few issues (as most do)." As time went on things began to completely make sense and it became apparent that this really was a sick church. Don't get me wrong, the pastor is a good man who loves God; he believes in the

> gifts, but does not use them or really allow them in the church unless they are very controlled. As it turned out, there were a lot of problems just under the surface.

For as long as she can remember, nightmares have always been a part of Eiko's life. She became a night owl, thinking that if she was very, very tired, then she could perhaps sleep through the night but, of course, that didn't work out so well. She had no idea how to stop the frightening dreams, or any concept that there could be some meaning behind them aside from torment. She continues:

> I participated in *Unraveling the Mysteries of Dream Interpretation* over the Internet in 2013, and it gave me an understanding of how dreams worked. I gained hope that my nightmares would stop one day. The audience was given the opportunity to submit dream examples if one wanted an interpretation so I submitted mine, just a piece of what I would see each night. It caught Barbara's attention, and she advised me to make an appointment to work with her for deeper healing because no one should be tormented like this. The first private session revealed that misogyny existed in my family line, and my journey for deeper healing began. Misogyny, rejection and abandonment ran deep in my spirit, soul and body, and it took some generational work to be healed from that. This is now 2017, and I can say that my nightmare time is over, and my dreams are beginning to do what they were designed to do—reveal deeper things that I am not aware of otherwise.
>
> I find it fascinating that dreams are like parables tailored personally for me in regard to my situation, and as I press in with the Lord, the interpretation comes. Recently, a dream revealed an unresolved emotional issue dating back to when I was approximately 16 years old. I had complained to the Lord a number of times about a past problem that continued into my current life, and an answer came through the dream that I needed to have deeper healing in order to rebuild a damaged relationship

> with my father. This revelation and subsequent healing contributed tremendously to revitalizing the relationship with my father and the outlook of my life.
>
> We know in our minds that the Lord is the God of restoration, and dreams can take us to that very experience of how God reveals, heals and restores us to the deeper and new levels of freedom that we would not have known otherwise. It is important to pay attention to the dreams we have, and press in with the Lord for interpretation. If we just let the dream go, we may also let our opportunity for freedom go.

Selina's testimony illustrates not only the faithfulness of God but also the wisdom of seeking Him first and of receiving wise counsel when help is needed with Dreamspeak:

> God has spoken to me through dreams for as long as I can remember. Most of the time I understand the meaning of my dreams, but during a particularly difficult time in my life when I was seeking God for guidance I had a dream that I couldn't understand. I knew in my spirit that this dream was an answer to what I had been in prayer about, so I received help from a seasoned dream interpreter. It was in fact, one of those dreams that altered the course of my life in a mighty way. Not only life changing, but it also lifted up and helped me walk through the valley. I shared it with my prayer partner and we cried tears of joy for the things God revealed through that dream. Not everything in it has come to pass, but I continue to hold on to the promises of God. He is so faithful and good to His children, and I'm glad he speaks to me through dreams.

How has your life changed as a result of understanding your dreams? Have you too experienced deliverance, healing or encouragement from God through dreams? Perhaps your testimony will also encourage someone else! Ideally, everyone should have a good story to tell once Dreamspeak becomes a natural part of everyday life.

Practical Application:
Keep a record of how dream interpretations have blessed or changed your life so you will never forget what God has done, and so you can share your story, encouraging others with your testimony.

[1] Acts 4:33

CHAPTER TWENTY-FIVE

WARNING! HANDLE WITH CARE

When is the last time you read all the warnings enclosed with a new purchase? It would seem that in our litigious society, every manufacturer feels compelled to warn of every conceivable risk, whether serious or mundane. Who doesn't understand that anything with an electrical cord poses a risk of electrical shock if you use it in the bathtub? And who doesn't know that household cleaners should be kept out of the reach of children? In November 2016, the *Harvard Business Review* reported that consumer warnings are not working because they fail overwhelmingly to distinguish between large and small risks.[1]

The Bible is also full of warnings but unlike marketers' advisories, every one of them should be heeded seriously; God's word can never be taken lightly. But perhaps we've come to treat some of God's warnings with as little respect as we do consumer alerts because we've become immune to them. How could that happen? The reasons vary, but easily include compromise when we decide that little sins are OK. Maybe we even justify the big sins because, "everybody else does it so it must be OK"; or perhaps we've fallen into the trap of using God's grace as an excuse for bad behavior. Whatever the reason, it's always a very foolish idea to neglect God's standards of righteousness—His warning labels, so to speak.

When it comes to dreams, the Bible almost screams, "Handle with care," and wisdom dictates a healthy fear of the Lord:

> *Be not rash with your mouth, nor let your heart be hasty to utter a word before God, for God is in heaven and you are on earth. Therefore let your words be few. For a dream comes with much business, and a fool's voice with many words…For when dreams increase and words grow many, there is vanity; but God is the one you must fear.*[2]

Let us not be found guilty of using dreams as a means of justifying sin:

> *Yet in like manner these people also, relying on their dreams, defile the flesh, reject authority, and blaspheme the glorious ones.*[3]

We live in a day that the Apostle Peter's quote from Joel seems timely:

> *And in the last days it shall be, God declares, that I will pour out my Spirit on all flesh, and your sons and your daughters shall prophesy, and your young men shall see visions, and your old men shall dream dreams; even on my male servants and female servants in those days I will pour out my Spirit, and they shall prophesy.*[4]

Another end-times prophecy that goes hand-in-hand with this promised outpouring is sobering. Jesus warned:

> *For false christs and false prophets will arise and perform great signs and wonders, so as to lead astray, if possible, even the elect.*[5]

A familiar verse of an old song from childhood days in Sunday School or Vacation Bible School offers some wise advice that can easily be applied to the way we speak about our dreams:

> O be careful little mouth what you say
> O be careful little mouth what you say
> There's a Father up above
> And He's looking down in love
> So, be careful little mouth what you say

Dreams are subject to interpretation, and a correct understanding must always align with scripture. Not only that, but there must also be an assurance from the Holy Spirit that this is what the Father is saying at the moment to avoid misapplying a valid truth out of context or prematurely. Not all dreams should be spoken of immediately, even when correctly understood, and the Lord's direction must be clearly discerned before making prophetic declarations. Remember the trouble Joseph got himself into when he spoke too soon about his God-given dreams?

> *Now Joseph had a dream, and when he told it to his brothers they hated him even more. He said to them, "Hear this dream that I*

have dreamed: Behold, we were binding sheaves in the field, and behold, my sheaf arose and stood upright. And behold, your sheaves gathered around it and bowed down to my sheaf." His brothers said to him, "Are you indeed to reign over us? Or are you indeed to rule over us?" So they hated him even more for his dreams and for his words.

Then he dreamed another dream and told it to his brothers and said, "Behold, I have dreamed another dream. Behold, the sun, the moon, and eleven stars were bowing down to me." But when he told it to his father and to his brothers, his father rebuked him and said to him, "What is this dream that you have dreamed? Shall I and your mother and your brothers indeed come to bow ourselves to the ground before you?" And his brothers were jealous of him, but his father kept the saying in mind.

We know that ultimately Joseph's prophetic dreams were fulfilled, but not before his brothers sold him into slavery. Then, just when things seemed to be going well, he was falsely accused and thrown into prison. [6] Fortunately, this time it was Joseph's ability to interpret dreams that got him out of trouble.[7] Still, it was only after twenty-three years of painful separation from his family, hidden guilt on the part of his brothers, and hopeless grief over a son thought to be dead by his father, did the brothers finally bow down to Joseph, not just once but on five different occasions. [8] Just because young Joseph's dreams were from God and the obvious interpretation seemed exciting, it's clear that his haste to share them wasn't the wisest decision he ever made! His story beautifully illustrates the truth that God does cause all things to work together for good for those who love Him are called according to His purpose.[9]

Additionally, we must beware of false dreams—dreams of deception—that are attempts to distort God's truth either in our own lives or the lives of others. How sad if we choose to listen to a false message and are deceived; how sad if our faith is built on lies:

Your prophets have seen for you false and deceptive visions; they have not exposed your iniquity to restore your fortunes, but have seen for you oracles that are false and misleading.[10]

Teaching or prophesying based on dreams that are not of God immediately place one into the false prophet category of which Jesus warned; definitely not a good place to be! Hundreds of years before Jesus, God spoke through both Jeremiah and Ezekiel about the dire consequences of hearing or proclaiming false prophecies:

> *Thus says the LORD of hosts: "Do not listen to the words of the prophets who prophesy to you, filling you with vain hopes. They speak visions of their own minds, not from the mouth of the LORD...I have heard what the prophets have said who prophesy lies in my name, saying, 'I have dreamed, I have dreamed!' How long shall there be lies in the heart of the prophets who prophesy lies, and who prophesy the deceit of their own heart, who think to make my people forget my name by their dreams that they tell one another, even as their fathers forgot my name for Baal? Let the prophet who has a dream tell the dream, but let him who has my word speak my word faithfully. What has straw in common with wheat? declares the LORD...Behold, I am against those who prophesy lying dreams, declares the LORD, and who tell them and lead my people astray by their lies and their recklessness, when I did not send them or charge them. So they do not profit this people at all, declares the LORD...And I will bring upon you everlasting reproach and perpetual shame, which shall not be forgotten.'"*[11]

> *"They have seen false visions and lying divinations. They say, 'Declares the Lord,' when the Lord has not sent them, and yet they expect him to fulfill their word. Have you not seen a false vision and uttered a lying divination, whenever you have said, 'Declares the Lord,' although I have not spoken?" Therefore thus says the Lord God: "Because you have uttered falsehood and seen lying visions, therefore behold, I am against you, declares the Lord God. My hand will be against the prophets who see false visions and who give lying divinations. They shall not be in the council of my people, nor be enrolled in the register of the house of Israel, nor shall they enter the land of Israel. And you shall know that I am the Lord God."*[12]

Manipulating people through dreams is an ancient deceptive tool, which the enemy is proficient at using to draw people away from God. If the old adage that 'practice makes perfect' could be applied to the devil and his cohorts, it would be easy to imagine that their evil techniques have only been enhanced over the years since Moses shared God's warning with the Israelites:

> *"If a prophet or a dreamer of dreams arises among you and gives you a sign or a wonder, and the sign or wonder that he tells you comes to pass, and if he says, 'Let us go after other gods,' which you have not known, 'and let us serve them,' you shall not listen to the words of that prophet or that dreamer of dreams. For the Lord your God is testing you, to know whether you love the Lord your God with all your heart and with all your soul. You shall walk after the Lord your God and fear him and keep his commandments and obey his voice, and you shall serve him and hold fast to him. But that prophet or that dreamer of dreams shall be put to death, because he has taught rebellion against the Lord your God, who brought you out of the land of Egypt and redeemed you out of the house of slavery, to make you leave the way in which the Lord your God commanded you to walk. So you shall purge the evil from your midst."* [13]

The biblical warnings regarding false prophets are many, and none end well for the person guilty of spreading deception. Before we begin shouting our dreams and interpretations from any rooftops, we would be well advised to heed God's warnings and study to show ourselves approved[14] in regard to Dreamspeak.

Practical Application:

Review the practical applications in the Appendix and pray about how to apply them in your life. Continue to study both the scriptures and other dream resources as led by the Lord. Carefully consider and pray about how to include your dreams as you teach or minister to others.

[1] https://hbr.org/2016/11/consumer-warning-labels-arent-working

[2] Ecclesiastes 5: 2-3, 7

[3] Jude 1:8

[4] Acts 2:17-18

[5] Matthew 24:24

[6] Genesis 39

[7] Genesis 40-41

[8] Genesis 42:6-7; 43:26, 28; 44:14-16; 50:18

[9] Romans 8:28

[10] Lamentations 2:14

[11] Jeremiah 23:16, 25-28, 32, 40

[12] Ezekiel 13:6-9

[13] Deuteronomy 13:1-5

[14] 2 Timothy 2:15

CHAPTER TWENTY-SIX
CONCLUSION

We must ponder and pray into the mysteries experienced though dreams and visions, and also study the scriptures to confirm what we think we already know. As we do, the Holy Spirit will lead us into previously unimaginable heights and depths of the knowledge and wisdom of God. Even as He teaches us of His mysterious ways, He also downloads such things as comfort, encouragement, instruction, peace and rest, as He converses with us in ways that cannot be understood by those who do not love the Lord. What a privilege and honor it is to understand that God cares for us so much that He loves to impart His wisdom and knowledge in this manner!

Months ago, this work began with a whisper from the Lord to write about dreams, followed by my agreement to do so as long as He would inspire a discussion that was different than mainstream resources for dream interpretation. At the time, I had no clue about how to proceed, but then He led me to make it about how He did it with me and ideas started flowing. There were some long stretches when there was no inspiration or inclination to continue, and the computer file remained closed for weeks on end; but then a new breeze of the Spirit would blow, and off we'd go again.

From the beginning, my hope has been to provide a framework to the Body of Christ that goes beyond interpretation and takes the dreamer into the experiential exploration of the heavenly realms. My continuing prayer is that God will use this book (after all, it was His idea in the first place!) to encourage His kids to step into His creative and personally designed language of Dreamspeak.

Once again, happy dreaming!!!

APPENDIX 1: PRAYER TO RELEASE DREAMS

On behalf of my entire generational line and myself, I renounce and repent for all of us who ever discounted or ignored our God-given dreams.

I repent for all who have: believed or said, "I never dream," or "God doesn't speak through dreams"; discouraged, mocked and/or shut down the dreams of others in any way, especially those of children; received and believed false dreams and/or dream interpretations; become false prophets or teachers based on dreams.

I now break all self-curses that I have made in regard to dreams, and in the name of Jesus I command all dream-blocking spirits to leave and go to the feet of Jesus. I also command the fear of dreaming and all deception, including religious spirits and false prophecy, to leave and go to the feet of Jesus.

Lord Jesus, will you now close all of the unrighteous doors that have been opened against my dreams and open the doors of righteousness. I invite you to possess the gates of my dreams, come into them, live in them, and speak Your truth into my heart and mind. Please increase my discernment, grant me Your wisdom and knowledge, and teach me to understand my dreams. Your promise in John 14:26 states:

> *But the Helper, the Holy Spirit, whom the Father will send in My name, He will teach you all things, and bring to your remembrance all that I said to you.*

Will you now, please fulfill that promise in my life in regard to dreams, visions, and twilight experiences?

In Jesus' name, amen.

APPENDIX 2: MAKING IT PRACTICAL SUMMARY (NUMBERS CORRESPOND TO CHAPTERS)

1. Start identifying your personal Dreamspeak vocabulary by writing down your observations, including such things as symbols, people who appear, repetitious dreams, common themes, and anything else that occurs to you.

2. Pursue intimacy with God as relentlessly as you would pursue a potential love interest. Talk to Him, walk with Him, listen to Him; learn to recognize and understand His voice any time of the day or night, whether awake or asleep.

3. Ponder and pray about dream encounters with an unidentified man (often, the Lord) to determine if you have had one-on-one conversations with God while you slept.

4. Begin learning your own personal dream language by recording your dreams and symbols and praying about what they mean to you. God is actually speaking all of the time if we pay attention; so throughout each day, consider the question about the circumstances you encounter, "If this was a dream, what would it mean?"

5. Consider the dimensionality of your dreams. Where have you gone? What have you experienced? Did your experience seem historical or futuristic?

6. Develop a habit of writing down your dreams as soon as you wake up.

7. Write down any vivid dreams that you have never forgotten, and begin praying about what they might mean. Also, even if a dream seems like one you will never, ever, forget; write it down anyway because you just might.

8. Record any recurring dreams that you've had and do not yet understand.

9. Take the who/what/where/when/why queries about your dreams to the Lord before diving into other resources. If there is no clear response, pray for His direction as you begin your research.

10. Begin to identify the resources for your own 'research library'. That God should be first on the list is a given; but next, identify printed materials, online helps, audio-visual presentations, seminars, and think about what people you know who can assist you in the quest to interpret your dreams. Ask the Lord to guide you to the resources that are best for you.

11. Pay careful attention to moments between sleep and wakefulness, and make a note of anything heard, seen or sensed. Later, when fully awake, ponder and pray into the twilight experience to fully grasp the meaning of what God was communicating.

12. Ask the Lord to reveal His view of what you see in your dreams and study scriptures that illustrate His omniscience, omnipotence, and omnipresence. Ask Him to show you how your dreams express His perspective. Thank Him for confirmations and instruction that comes through others.

13. Consider the difficult questions you may have about dreams and then search out biblical principles that may apply to them.

14. Continue to pursue intimacy with God, learning to recognize His voice. Pursue your own healing through deliverance, personal payer and Bible study so that the improving condition of your heart will be reflected in your dreams, and so you cannot be easily deceived.

15. Pay attention to physical sensations within dreams and consider what that discernment could mean and how God wants you to use it to do what the Father is doing.

16. Review your dreams to identify difficult situations in which you find yourself. Ask the Lord to show you what he wants you to know; try to interpret what the symbols mean; if necessary,

contact a trusted friend or a prayer minister to help you receive the deliverance that the Lord wants to administer.

17. Consider ways in which the events of your daily life may interact with and/or be impacted by your dreams. Ponder the question, "If this was a dream, what would it mean?"

18. Pray for unbelievers to experience dreams and visions that will lead them into a relationship with God. When a non-Christian appears in your dreams, consider how God might be leading you to pray for or minister to them.

19. Consider instances when the Jesus may have shown up in your dreams as well as times when there was an unidentified individual, the Holy Spirit, in the background. What were they doing? Consider the significance of seeing the Lord in a dream. How does it change your outlook on life?

20. Think about dreams in which you received guidance or encouragement. Journal the difference those dreams made in your life and spend some time thanking and praising God for His intervention.

21. Be careful not to assume a textbook interpretation is correct, regardless of the type of dream. Always, always, ask the Lord first and prayerfully consider the message in every dream.

22. Try to recognize Dreamspeak clues indicating that you've gone somewhere outside of the time indicated on your alarm clock. Have you gone backward or forward, or are you outside of time looking in from another dimension? Do you recognize a setting, experience, or individual that you know you've never encountered before in the physical realm?

23. Begin a list of your own reflections about Dreamspeak. Include insights as well as questions you'd like to have answered. Then, talk to the Lord about it; research your questions just as you would a particular dream; and ask trusted friends for assistance.

24. Keep a record of how dream interpretations have blessed or

changed your life so you will never forget what God has done and so you can share your story, encouraging others with your testimony.

25. Review the practical applications above and pray about how to apply them in your life. Continue to study both the scriptures and other dream resources as led by the Lord. Carefully consider and pray about how to include your dreams as you teach or minister to others.

RECOMMENDED RESOURCES

The Holy Spirit, first and foremost, closely followed by ***The Holy Bible***

Unraveling the Mystery of Dream Interpretation, by Barbara Parker, is a four-hour seminar that was recorded at Aslan's Place, which includes comprehensive information regarding dreams as well as explanations of real dreams that were submitted by the audience. For more information, see: http://aslansplace.com/language/en/unraveling-the-mystery-of-dream-interpretation-barbara-parker/

The Divinity Code, by Adrian Beale and Adam F. Thompson, is a wonderful, all-inclusive book that provides a biblical understanding of dreams and visions, practice interpretations, and an extensive metaphor dictionary. Additionally, appendices and subject indexes make it easy to locate specific information.

Understand Your Dream Now: Spiritual Dream Interpretation, by Doug Addison, is an excellent, compact, how-to-interpret dreams book.

If This Were a Dream, What Would It Mean? by Murray Dueck, is a book that encourages the reader to learn to look at everyday events as if they were dreams in order to begin to understand more of what God is doing.

The Dictionary of Biblical Imagery, edited by Leland Ryken, James C. Wilhoit and Tremper Longman III, explores images, symbols, motifs, metaphors, figures of speech, and literary patterns of the Bible.

The Prophet's Dictionary, by Paula A. Price, Ph.D., is a reference book containing over 1,600 terms and phrases that are relevant to the prophetic realm.

Internet Search Engines are very helpful to research words, names, places, people, etc. who appear in a dream.